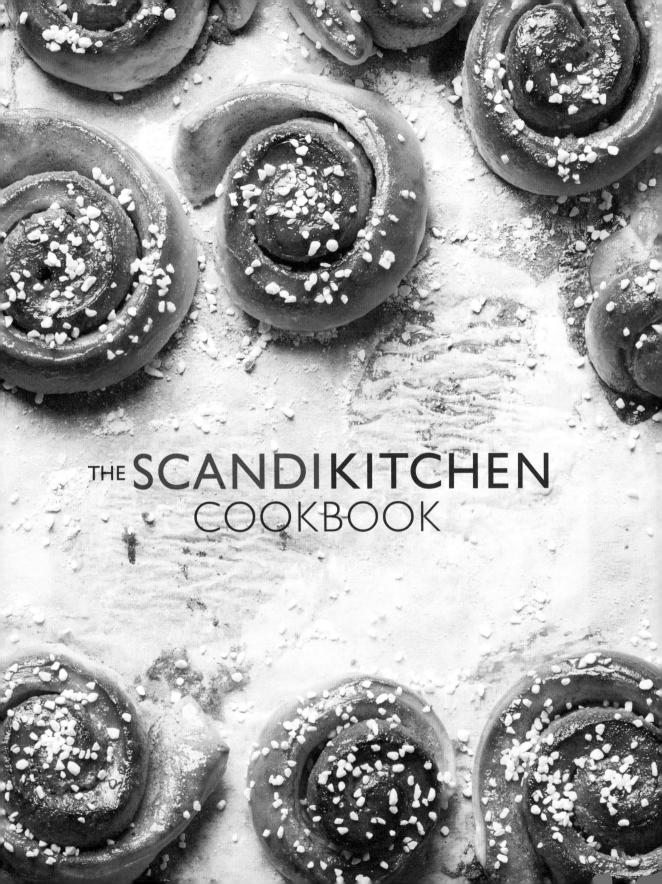

THE SCANDIKITCHEN
COOKBOOK

THE SCANDIKITCHEN
COOKBOOK

Recipes for good food with love from Scandinavia

BRONTË AURELL

Photography by Peter Cassidy

RYLAND PETERS & SMALL
LONDON • NEW YORK

For Jonas, Astrid and Elsa – always, with all my love x

Senior Designer Sonya Nathoo
Commissioning Editor Nathan Joyce
Head of Production Patricia Harrington
Creative Director Leslie Harrington
Editorial Director Julia Charles
Publisher Cindy Richards

Food Stylists Bridget Sargeson and
Jack Sargeson
Prop Stylist Linda Berlin
Indexer Vanessa Bird

First published in the United Kingdom
in 2015 by Ryland Peters & Small
20–21 Jockey's Fields
London WC1R 4BW
and
341 East 116th Street
New York NY 10029
www.rylandpeters.com

Text © Bronte Aurell 2015, 2024
(recipes on pages 37, 56, and 59
written in partnership with Kobi Ruzicka)
Design and photographs
© Ryland Peters & Small 2015, 2024

ISBN: 978-1-78879-599-9

10 9 8 7 6 5 4 3 2 1

The author's moral rights have been asserted.
All rights reserved. No part of this publication
may be reproduced, stored in a retrieval
system, or transmitted in any form or by any
means, electronic, mechanical, photocopying
or otherwise, without the prior permission of
the publisher.

Printed and bound in China.

CIP data from the Library of Congress has
been applied for. A CIP record for this book
is available from the British Library.

Notes
• Both British (metric) and American
(imperial plus US cups) are included in these
recipes; however, it is important to work with one
set of measurements and not alternate between
the two within a recipe.
• All spoon measurements are level unless
otherwise specified.
• All eggs are medium (UK) or large (US), unless
specified as large, in which case US extra large
should be used. Uncooked or partially cooked
eggs should not be served to the very old, frail,
young children, pregnant women or those with
compromised immune systems.
• Ovens should be preheated to the specified
temperatures. We recommend using an oven
thermometer. If using a fan-assisted oven, adjust
temperatures according to the manufacturer's
instructions.
• When a recipe calls for the grated zest of citrus
fruit, buy unwaxed fruit and wash well before
using. If you can only find treated fruit, scrub
well in warm soapy water before using.

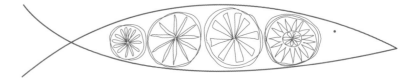

CONTENTS

HEJ AND WELCOME TO SCANDIKITCHEN

We first had the idea for ScandiKitchen in a ski lodge on a Swedish mountain in 2006. It was the last day of holidays and we had to go back to London. We were discussing what food we needed to stuff into our checked plane luggage (and if we could get away with wearing any of these items as a hat), because there were very few places in the UK where we get hold of Scandi foods and where we could go and be 'Scandinavian' with our friends. So, if noone else was going to make a place like that, then why shouldn't we?

The idea for ScandiKitchen was never about being fancy. It was about making the food we miss from home and introducing it to the people around us: *Good Food With Love From Scandinavia*. In the eight years we've been open, this is still the principle behind every single thing we do. From the open sandwiches we make in the café, to the groceries we stock in the shop and online, and the amazing people who choose to work with us... Everything comes down to being honest about who we are, how we eat and being able to proudly say: We eat this at home and we think it's really nice – try it.

The run-up to opening day was a bit of a blur. Everything was done on a shoestring and we worked so hard trying to get everything ready in time. This was mainly due to a huge time limit on things, as Brontë was pregnant with our first child and the due date was fast approaching. Opening day – Tuesday 10th July, 2007 – was hot and humid, and we worried that nobody would come. But they did – and we were busy and bustling for the whole day. We closed the shop in the early evening, cleaned up, locked the door and drove to the hospital to say hello to baby Astrid, who arrived considerately just after midnight. Jonas slept in a chair at the hospital and went back to open the shop the next morning at 7am. It was a harsh welcome to the life of café ownership.

The café has gone from strength to strength, despite the economic climate. A few years later, we added a web-shop and wholesale to the business and moved Jonas out to the warehouse (a place we named 'StockHome', obviously). Today, ScandiKitchen supplies Scandinavian food to the whole of the UK and parts of continental Europe, too.

We love that our customers are a mix of Scandinavian expats, people who have Scandinavian ancestry, and local people just interested in different and good food. We welcome everybody, and we genuinely want to know about the food you're missing from home or the Scandi recipe you're trying out for the first time.

Being busy is good, but it also means we sometimes don't get to sit down and talk about baking or cooking with everybody as much as we'd like. Our customers and friends have asked us for years to write down our recipes and tell our story, so here it is. The recipes in this book are honest and they are how we make food at home and at the café. Nothing complicated or fancy, just simple *Good Food With Love From Scandinavia*. We hope you enjoy it.

Brontë and Jonas X

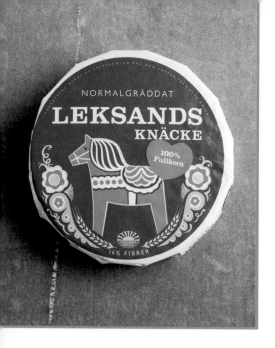

THE SCANDI PANTRY

Here is a small guide to some of the products you may find in a Scandinavian pantry today. It is by no means a complete list – Scandinavia is over 2,500 km/1,550 miles from top to bottom – and our pantry varies from region to region. We have included notes on some of the ingredients most commonly found across the countries, and those we get a lot of questions about at the café. Being an authentic expat shop, we often help people to find the exact ingredient for their particular recipes. You'll find a comprehensive list of products on our website at www.scandikitchen.co.uk

HERBS AND SPICES

Allspice
Used in minced/ground meat dishes, such as meatballs. Usually bought ground, but you can buy the dried berries and grind them at home.

Caraway seeds
These often feature in bread, and many of our cheeses use them as a flavouring.

Cardamom
Vikings first sampled this aromatic spice during their raids on Constantinople. It's used mainly in baked goods and cakes. The recipes in this book are made using pre-ground cardamom, which loses potency quickly once opened, so adjust accordingly. Alternatively, shell cardamom pods to grind your own. Bear in mind that if you do grind your own, you'll need to adjust to a lower quantity, as it is so much more potent. You can buy cardamom seeds ready-shelled in speciality shops.

Cinnamon
Cinnamon is used extensively in Scandinavian baking. It is worth opting for a good-quality ground cinnamon rather than buying cheap cinnamon powder.

Cloves
Used in Christmas baking and cooking – and in Glögg, aka Nordic mulled wine. Ground cloves feature in our ginger biscuits.

Curry
In Danish cooking, and some Norwegian and Swedish dishes, mild curry powder is used (Meatballs in Curry Sauce, and Curried Herring, to name but two dishes). Danes have been using curry powder for at least the past 100 years in several traditional dishes. It's never spicy and you sometimes have to add ground turmeric to increase the desired yellow colouring.

Dill (fresh)
Used in many fish dishes. We also use crown dill (dill that has been allowed to flower) when cooking crayfish in August. We usually favour fresh dill, although dill seeds and dried dill are also used. Dill is also used to flavour aquavit.

Fennel seeds
Used in bread baking – both in crispbread and other breads.

Ginger (dried)
We usually use ground ginger in our Christmas baking. Pieces of dried whole ginger are sometimes used in our mulled wine.

Juniper berries

Often used in game dishes. They're great with reindeer and venison.

Liquorice

We use liquorice powder, syrup and root for baking and general cooking. Look for high-quality syrups and powders such as 'Lakrids by Bülow' – they cost more, but will improve the end result immensely.

Saffron

Swedes love using saffron at Christmas in baking – we rarely use it in savoury cooking. You often find powdered saffron in Swedish supermarkets. You can use the strands, too – but you have to grind them finely before using in baking. To intensify the colour, soak in the warm liquid specified in the recipe before using.

Salt

For centuries, our diet has utilized salt to preserve our fish and meats, and it is said that this is why Scandinavians often have a taste for anything salty. Our love of all things salty means we even like salt on our liquorice.

Seville orange peel

Seville orange is bitter, and we use this at Christmas time for Glögg and for baking speciality Christmas breads. If you can't get Seville orange, substitute with other dried orange peel, but note that the result will be less subtle in flavour.

Star anise

We use it in both sweet and savoury cooking.

Vanilla

We use a lot of real vanilla, but we mostly use vanilla sugar (rarely extract), which looks a bit like icing/confectioners' sugar. You can make it at home by adding 150 g/1 cup of icing/confectioners' sugar to a small food processor with a dried-out vanilla pod/bean. Pulse until completely pulverised, then sift out the large pieces of pod/bean. You can buy vanilla sugar in Scandinavian food shops.

BERRIES

Cloudberries (bakeapple)

It's near impossible to buy fresh cloudberries and frozen ones fetch a very high price (around £40/$64 per kg). The cloudberry is hard to cultivate – people who forage for it know the best patches and they definitely don't kiss and tell. On top of that, cloudberries grow on stalks and break easily. If you are lucky enough to find someone who is a cloudberry forager, make him your best friend immediately. Most cloudberries are turned into jam, which is considered a gourmet item; for that reason, we don't spread it on toast, but use it in desserts and with cheese. It's hard to substitute – a very tart raspberry is closest.

Lingonberries

You will find whole lingonberries in our freezers and most likely a version of lingonberry jam in our store cupboard. We use frozen or fresh lingonberries for both sweet and savoury dishes. The jam is most often used together with meat dishes. It's rarely used as a jam on toast.

VEGETABLES

Asier

A Danish speciality food, asier is a type of cucumber which is peeled and pickled. It's often served with Christmas pork and on liver pâté.

Pickled beetroot

We use sliced pickled beet(root) in salads, as a side dish to meals and on our open sandwiches. Nordic pickled beet(root) tends to be sweeter than others, so you may need to add sugar for a comparable taste.

Pickled cucumber

You'll find various types of sliced pickled cucumbers in our cupboards. It's used as a side dish or as a sandwich topping. Lightly pickled cucumber salad (soused cucumber) is more commonly used in Denmark.

Wild mushrooms

Dried wild mushrooms are used, especially in Swedish cooking. We use fresh whenever we can, but during seasons where fresh ones do not make it, we may use dried or even canned. We most often use 'Kantareller' (chanterelles) and 'Karl Johan' (porcini).

FISH

Ansjovis

The Swedes are to blame for the confusion around this ingredient: many years ago, they named a tin of sprats in brine 'Ansjovis' – despite not being anchovies at all. They are silver-bellied and blue-green on the sides like their Mediterranean brothers, but the end result is a spicier and sweeter one rather than salty. The famous dish Jansson's Temptation (see page 84) has been ruined by many people substituting 'Ansjovis' for anchovies. The 'Ansjovis' sprats are much more like pickled herring than Mediterranean anchovies – so if you need to substitute, use herring instead. Store these tins in the refrigerator. You can get the real deal at any Scandinavian food store, even those selling bookshelves.

Herring

Eaten all across the Nordic countries, Atlantic herring is one of our staples. We pickle it, smoke it, cure it, fry it – it is a delicious fish, high in omega-3 fats. It comes both canned and in jars, but do store them in the refrigerator.

OILS, VINEGARS AND MUSTARD

Ättika 24%

This Swedish vinegar is very strong and you dilute with water accordingly. Many Scandinavian pickling recipes will specify the percentage you need to pickle your produce in (5–6% for vegetables, 12% for herring and so on). It's near impossible to find in supermarkets/grocery stores in the UK/US, but it can be bought in speciality shops.

Mustards

Scandinavians favour sweet, strong mustards. You can substitute with the grainy Dijon mustard in recipes, although, you may need to add sugar. Scandinavian mustards are rather good and if you happen to come across a stash, do stock up.

Rapeseed oil (canola oil)

Rapeseed oil is traditionally used in Scandinavian cooking – it's local and it has less saturated fat than olive oil. However, cheap rapeseed oil is not great so don't go buying an inferior brand instead of using other good-quality oils you may already have.

FLOUR AND GRAINS

Crispbread

There are more types of crispbread than there is space to mention. We use the healthier fibre/high wholemeal or high-rye ones for day-to-day use and the sweeter, wheat-based ones for treats. We enjoy crispbread for breakfast and lunch. It's not a diet bread, though.

Malt

Barley malt is important in Danish bread baking. You can buy malt protein powder online at bakery speciality stores. You can also use barley malt extract from health food stores. We also drink something called Hvidtøl, a low-alcohol malt beer used in many older Nordic recipes, which can also be used in bread baking.

Oats

Used for porridge, granola, muesli, baking – and we also eat them raw with milk for breakfast.

Oat flakes (jumbo oats) or cut oats are favoured. We rarely use oatmeal.

Potato flour
Many Scandinavian recipes call for the use of potato flour (potato starch). You can buy this in speciality stores. Once potato starch is added, the dish should not boil (especially in fruit-based sauces as these will go cloudy after boiling). Substitute with cornflour/cornstarch for general cooking, although not in baking.

Rye
There are two types of rye grains available: the whole grain and the cut one (kibbled or cracked rye). I use whole rye grains for salads. The cracked rye is for bread. The two are not really interchangeable: if you bake with the whole grain, it can be hard to bite into the bread. If you cook the cracked one in salads, the result is sticky. If you cannot find cracked rye for your bread, use whole but pulse briefly in your food processor (or even pre-boil it).

Rye flakes
I love using rye flakes in granolas and porridge (mixed with normal oats). It has a nutty flavour and a good bite. Available in health food stores.

Rye flour
We use light rye and dark coarse rye flours in our baking. In this book, recipes are made using the standard dark rye.

Semolina
Used for some desserts and also as a porridge.

Spelt
Spelt is a type of wheat. Known as 'dinkel' in Swedish, spelt is an old grain and a cousin of the wheat we know today. Use spelt grains cooked in salads or spelt flour in your baking. You can substitute normal wheat flour with spelt flour, but I do think mixing it half and half gives a nicer result. Spelt contains gluten – but generally lower counts than other wheat.

OTHER

Baker's ammonia
Old Nordic recipes often call for baker's ammonia (ammonium bicarbonate), known to us as Hjortetakssalt/Hjorthornssalt. It's a leavening agent used to make biscuits extra crispy. Substitute with bicarbonate of/baking soda/powder, although the result will not be as crispy. Note that baker's ammonia gives a very strong ammonia smell as you bake but this disappears as soon as the biscuit cools.

Dried/active dry yeast
These are little granules you have to activate in lukewarm water before using.

Fresh or compressed yeast
25 g/1 oz. of fresh yeast is the equivalent to 13 g/½ oz. of dried/active dry yeast. It usually comes in packs of 50 g/2 oz. (usually) and looks a bit like clay.

Instant dried yeast
If you have no option but to use instant dried yeast (a fine powder sold in sachets), skip the liquid step and add to the dry ingredients. Follow the manufacturer's guidelines for the equivalent measure.

DRINKS

Aquavit
Grain- or potato-based spirit, usually containing around 38–40% alcohol. Common flavour notes are caraway, aniseed and dill. It's always served ice-cold in small shot glasses, together with pickled herring, or at crayfish parties.

Punch
A type of Swedish rum liquor, often used to flavour rum truffle treats such as 'Dammsugare' (see page 173). You can substitute it for good concentrated rum flavourings in baked treats.

BREAKFAST

Everyday Scandinavian breakfasts are made up of
a smörgåsbord of little, simple good-for-you things,
from crispbread to berries, porridge/oatmeal, yogurt
and healthy cereals. On the weekend, our lazy late
morning brunches are filled with lighter breads and
lovely gourmet additions such as smoked ham, cured
salmon and elaborate fruit salads. Mamma was right:
it really is the most important meal of the day!

NORDIC HEART WAFFLES

These heart-shaped waffles are eaten all over the Nordic countries. We use a special heart-shaped waffle iron, giving the waffles their distinct shape, which you can get online, but it's also possible to make using a non-stick griddle pan.

2 eggs

350 ml/1⅓ cups whole milk

100 ml/½ cup Greek yogurt

350 g/2¾ cups plain/ all-purpose flour

100 g/½ cup caster/ granulated sugar

1 teaspoon baking powder

1 teaspoon bicarbonate of/ baking soda

1 teaspoon vanilla sugar (or use seeds from ½ pod/bean)

½ teaspoon ground cardamom (optional)

100 g/1 stick minus 1 tablespoon butter, melted, plus 50 g/3 tablespoons, for brushing

VANILLA SKYR/QUARK AND TART BERRIES TOPPING:

300 ml/1½ cups skyr (Icelandic cultured dairy product) or natural quark

½ vanilla pod/bean, seeds only

2 tablespoons icing/ confectioners' sugar

200 g/7 oz. mixed fresh berries

STRAWBERRY JAM AND VANILLA CREAM TOPPING:

300 ml/1¼ cups whipping cream

½ vanilla pod/bean, seeds only

1 teaspoon icing/ confectioners' sugar

MAKES 10–12

In a bowl, combine the eggs, milk and yogurt. Add all the dry ingredients and finally, add the melted butter. Whisk until you have a smooth batter, taking care not to over-beat. Leave to stand for at least 15 minutes before using.

Heat up the waffle iron and brush it lightly with melted butter. Add enough batter to the waffle iron to almost cover the surface (but not quite, or it will overspill), close the lid and cook until golden brown. This will take a couple of minutes. Repeat until all the batter is used. Note that as when making pancakes, the first one of the batch is never as good as the rest! Eat them immediately or they'll go soggy.

For the vanilla skyr/quark and tart berries topping, whip the skyr or quark for 1 minute with the vanilla seeds and sugar. Serve a dollop with each waffle and then sprinkle the berries on top. Note that skyr and quark are naturally sour in taste and you may want to add extra sugar to taste.

For the strawberry jam and vanilla cream topping, add the cold whipping cream to a bowl. Add the seeds from the vanilla pod/ bean and icing/confectioners' sugar. Whip until peaks form. Serve the cream and jam in bowls next to the waffles and let your guests help themselves (usually a tablespoon of jam per waffle is sufficient). During strawberry season, we omit the jam and serve it with freshly macerated strawberries instead. Other times, we replace the strawberry jam with cloudberry jam – a much tarter jam that perfectly complements the sweet vanilla cream.

The traditional Norwegian waffle topping is brown goat's cheese (brunost or geitost), which is available in speciality stores across the world. The distinctive brown colour comes from the milk sugars which are boiled (along with cream and whey), turning them into caramel. To serve, thinly slice slivers of the brown cheese and add to your waffle as soon as it comes out of the waffle iron, so that it melts slightly before eating.

RYE-BREAD PORRIDGE WITH SKYR AND TOASTED HAZELNUTS

This porridge, known as 'Øllebrød' in Danish, features in the Academy-Award-winning Danish movie Babette's Feast. It is a very old recipe for rye-bread porridge, and was originally a way to use leftover rye bread and drabs of beer, hence the name Øllebrød, which translates as 'bread and beer soup'. You can make it with a malt beer or ale, but it's just as nice made with water. Some people eat Øllebrød as a dessert, but I love it in the mornings. I also love not wasting food, and it is a great way to use up end bits of rye bread.

200 g/7 oz. dark rye bread, ideally not seeded

600 ml/2⅓ cups water

1 piece of unwaxed orange peel (2.5-cm/1-in. diameter)

½ teaspoon ground cinnamon

¼ teaspoon cocoa powder

40 g/3 tablespoons caster/granulated sugar

1–2 teaspoons orange juice

skyr or plain yogurt, toasted hazelnuts (roughly chopped) and fresh berries, to serve

SERVES 2–3

Cut the rye bread into small pieces, then add to a saucepan. Cover with the water. Leave to soak for at least 15 minutes (or overnight in the fridge).

Add the orange peel, cinnamon and cocoa and bring to the boil. Leave to simmer for around 15–20 minutes until all bread has dissolved and you are left with what looks like a very thick gravy. Remove the orange peel. Add the sugar (hold back a little bit in case you prefer a less sweet version). Add the orange juice (you can add a little more, to taste). There may be the odd lump of bread left – I quite like these, but you can push it through a sieve/strainer if you prefer a smoother version.

If you have used seeded rye bread, the seeds will still be present. You can pulse the mixture a few times in a food processor if you want a smoother consistency.

Serve hot with a dollop of skyr (or plain yogurt), toasted hazelnuts and fresh berries, such as blueberries or raspberries. If serving as a dessert, add double/heavy cream instead of yogurt.

OAT-RYE PORRIDGE WITH LINGONBERRIES

For me, there is no better way to start the day than a big steaming bowl of porridge/oatmeal. I'm not a fan of store-bought mixes full of sugar and added nasties, so we always make our own. At the café, we always use a base of both jumbo oats and rye flakes. It may take a little longer to cook, but the result is a wholesome and tasty porridge/oatmeal.

80 g/1 cup minus 1 tablespoon oats (use rolled/old-fashioned or jumbo oats or a mixture – but vary the cooking time, as the jumbo oats take longer to cook)

20 g/1 tablespoon rye flakes

225 ml/1 cup minus 1 tablespoon water

225 ml/1 cup minus 1 tablespoon whole milk

a pinch of salt

small knob/pat of butter (optional)

Stirred Lingonberries (see page 92), to serve

pumpkin and sunflower seeds, to serve

PORRIDGE PANCAKES:

250 g/9 oz. cooled porridge/oatmeal

1 egg

25 g/2 tablespoons plain/all-purpose flour

1 teaspoon vanilla sugar

1/2 teaspoon bicarbonate of/baking soda

a splash of milk or water

coconut oil or butter, for frying

fresh berries or other fruit and maple or apple syrup, to serve

SERVES 2 (BOTH RECIPES)

In a saucepan, boil the oats and rye in the water and milk. Simmer while continuously stirring for 5-7 minutes or until the oats and rye are cooked. Add a pinch of salt to taste. For extra creaminess, add a small knob/pat of butter and stir through.

Add a good dollop of Stirred Lingonberries (see page 92, but make half a portion and go easy on the sugar before stirring the berries, because you don't want an overly sweet porridge topping) for an extra healthy vitamin boost. You could also add a pinch of cinnamon or a drop of vanilla extract to the stirred lingonberries.

Top with pumpkin seeds and sunflower seeds, or sprinkle with other seeds of your choice.

Leftover Porridge Pancakes

Sometimes, there's porridge/oatmeal left over. Don't throw it out! Save it for the next day – it takes just a few minutes to whip up delicious, filling oat and rye pancakes. Our daughters Astrid and Elsa love these as a treat.

Mix the ingredients together until you have a solid batter. It needs to be a similar texture to your morning porridge/oatmeal.

Heat the oil or butter in a frying pan/skillet. When hot, add a small ladleful of batter and cook until browned on both sides. Serve with fresh berries or other fruit and a drizzle of maple or apple syrup.

SAVOURY DILL AND VÄSTERBOTTEN CHEESE MUFFINS

I like to make these for the mornings when I know I need to eat on the go. They take just a few minutes to stir together and are baked in double-quick time. By the time I hit the road, they have cooled down enough to eat. I like a subtle dill flavour – but if you like stronger flavours, feel free to add more. My kids like it when I add fried bacon pieces to the batter.

175 g/1 cup plus 3 tablespoons plain/all-purpose flour

50 g/3 tablespoons wholemeal/wholewheat flour

2½ teaspoons baking powder

1 teaspoon salt

275 ml/1 cup plus 2 tablespoons milk

1 egg

100 g/½ cup minus 1 tablespoon cottage cheese

75 g/6 tablespoons melted butter

50 g/3 tablespoons grated Västerbotten cheese or mature/sharp Cheddar, plus an extra handful for topping

½ teaspoon Dijon mustard

2 tablespoons freshly chopped dill

a few twists of freshly ground black pepper

6–8 cherry tomatoes

25 g/2 tablespoons sunflower seeds

MAKES 6–8

Preheat the oven to 200°C (400°F) Gas 6. Line a muffin pan with paper cases.

In a bowl, add the flours, baking powder and salt and stir.

Add all the other ingredients (except the tomatoes and sunflower seeds) and stir until incorporated.

Spoon into the muffin/cupcake cases. Press one cherry tomato into each muffin until almost covered and top with the remaining grated cheese and sunflower seeds.

Bake for around 20 minutes or until done (when a skewer comes out clean).

Note: If you cannot get hold of Västerbotten cheese, substitute it with a good mature/sharp Cheddar. I make these using tulip muffin/cupcake cases, which are bigger than normal muffin/cupcake cases, so you may find you have a bit of extra batter if using regular cases.

Perfect little savoury muffins for when breakfast just has to be on the go – or as a side dish for a Nordic brunch.

FIL AND FLINGOR

One of the most important items on the Nordic breakfast table is yogurt and similar cultured dairy products. In Sweden, most people start the day with soured milk products called A-fil and Filmjölk – referred to as 'fil'. During the last decade, the Icelandic cultured dairy product skyr has also made a return to the breakfast tables in many Nordic households. At the café shop, we sell many litres of all of these types of 'fil' a week. Flingor refers to 'flakes' – or in this context, the topping we add to the yogurt. It is super easy to make great toppings for your fil, yogurt or skyr. Here I've included a classic Nordic granola and Ymerdrys – a true Danish favourite.

'fil', yogurt or skyr, to serve

OAT & RYE GRANOLA:

175 g/2 cups rolled/old-fashioned oats

125 g/1 cup plus 2 tablespoons rye flakes

3 tablespoons dark brown sugar

1 teaspoon vanilla sugar

1/2 teaspoon salt

1 teaspoon ground cinnamon

1/4 teaspoon ground ginger

1/4 teaspoon ground cloves

60 ml/4 tablespoons vegetable oil

80 m/1/4 cup plus 2 teaspoons runny honey

200 g/7 oz. mixed nuts and seeds (flaxseeds/linseeds, sunflower seeds, pumpkin seeds, chopped almonds and hazelnuts)

blueberries, raspberries and chopped strawberries, to serve

YMERDRYS TOPPING:

200 g/7 oz. Nordic rye bread

2 tablespoons brown sugar, plus extra, to taste

handful of flaxseeds/linseeds (optional)

SERVES 6–8

Preheat the oven to 160°C (325°F) Gas 3.

In a bowl, combine the oats, rye flakes, sugars and salt – along with the spices. Mix until combined. Add the oil and honey and mix again until fully incorporated. Put the mixture into a deep baking tray, spread it out well and bake in the preheated oven for around 15–20 minutes until crisped up. Do give the mixture a stir once in a while, taking care not to let it go too brown.

Remove the granola from the oven and leave to cool. Stir from time to time as it will keep firming up as it cools. Add all the nuts and seeds, stir and either serve or store in an airtight container for up to 2 weeks.

Serve the granola with freshly chopped strawberries, blueberries and raspberries and use as a quick, nutritious topping for your 'fil', yogurt or skyr.

Alternatively, to make the Ymerdrys topping (which you'll find ready-made in Danish stores), first preheat the oven to 160°C (325°F) Gas 3. Blitz the bread and sugar in a food processor until it has a fine crumb consistency. Pop the mixture onto a baking sheet and bake in the preheated oven until completely dry, approximately 20-30 minutes, taking care not to burn it.

Some people prefer the final Ymerdrys to be lumpy, but I like a fine crumb so I always blitz it again in the food processor for a few seconds. The amount of sugar you add depends on how sweet you like your topping. Some store-bought Ymerdrys is 40 per cent sugar, but I tend to think 20 per cent is more than enough! For a healthier Ymerdrys, add a handful of flaxseeds/linseeds before you blitz it for the second time. Mix into your choice of fil, yogurt or skyr and add berries or other fresh fruit.

BREAKFAST OPEN SANDWICH

One of the simplest, yet most delicious, breakfasts I know. Choose your bread – dark toasted rye works well, as does a good wholemeal sourdough. I love adding Kalles Kaviar on this – it's a creamed cod roe paste popular in Sweden and Norway (it comes in a tube and you can get it in speciality shops).

2 large eggs

2 slices of light rye sourdough or dark seeded rye bread

2 ripe avocados

salt and freshly ground black pepper

a handful of watercress (optional)

1–2 teaspoons Kalles Kaviar

SERVES 2

Bring a saucepan half-filled with water to the boil. Crack both eggs into a cup. Once the water is at a simmer, swirl the water quickly with a whisk to create a vortex and carefully tip in the eggs into the middle. If your eggs are fresh, the egg white will coagulate quickly and settle into cooking. Leave to cook at a low simmer for 2–3 minutes for soft poached.

Meanwhile, toast the bread.

Slice the avocados in half and remove the stones. Using a spoon, scoop out the flesh and, using a fork, smash the avocado in a bowl and season with salt and pepper. Spread onto the toast so you have a good, thick layer (depending on the size of your avocados, you may not need all of the second one).

Remove the eggs from the water with a slotted spoon and allow to drain. Add some watercress on top of the avocado or on the side, as desired. Add the Kalles Kaviar and then place the poached egg on top. Season with salt and pepper and serve immediately.

The ever-popular breakfast updated with a little bit of traditional Scandinavian creamed cod roe.

Cuddle up in front of the
log fire, 'fika' and feel
cosy – and forget about
the cold outside.

OPEN SANDWICHES

If asked to pick my favourite dish from Scandinavia, the open sandwich would win. The combinations are endless – and you can make them super healthy or as indulgent treats. A knife and fork are essential as they don't work as a grab-and-go sandwich but, frankly, I love anything that makes us stop, take a break, sit down and talk to each other.

PICKLED HERRINGS 3 WAYS

No Smörgåsbord is complete without pickled herring, and every Nordic country has its favourite. If you are new to eating pickled herring, starting with one in a dressing, like the three versions below, is a good introduction.

MUSTARD HERRING (Senapssill):

2 tablespoons Swedish mustard (Skaansk Senap is good) or a good, grainy sweet mustard

1 teaspoon Dijon mustard

1 tablespoon caster/granulated sugar

2 tablespoons white wine vinegar

2 tablespoons double/heavy cream

1 tablespoon crème fraîche/sour cream

1 small shallot, finely chopped

salt and ground black pepper

100 ml/7 tablespoons vegetable oil

2 tablespoons chopped fresh dill

1 tablespoon chopped chives

220–300 g/8–10½ oz. (drained weight) plain pickled Scandinavian herring

SERVES 4

In a bowl, mix all the ingredients together (except the herring, oil and herbs).

Slowly pour in the oil while whisking continuously so that the sauce emulsifies.

Add the herbs and the herring. Leave to marinade for a few hours in the fridge, then serve, garnished with chives.

Enjoy with rye or crispbread.

BEETROOT HERRING (Sillröra):

250–300 g/9–10½ oz. (drained weight) plain pickled Scandinavian herring

8–10 slices of pickled beet(root), drained (reserve a few tablespoons of the juice)

1 apple, sliced, cored and chopped

1–2 potatoes, cooked and diced

½ red onion, chopped

1–2 pickled cucumbers, chopped

50 g/3 tablespoons crème fraîche/sour cream

50 g/3 tablespoons mayonnaise

1 teaspoon Dijon mustard

salt and ground black pepper

1 tablespoon chopped chives

4 boiled egg halves, to serve

SERVES 4

Add all the ingredients (except the eggs) together and stir.

Leave to marinade for a few hours in the fridge, then serve with buttered rye bread or crispbread.

Serve the boiled egg halves alongside the beetroot herring salad and top with chives.

CURRIED HERRING (Karrysild):

½ apple

1–2 gherkins/pickled cucumbers

½ red onion

1 teaspoon capers

1 teaspoon mild curry powder

½ teaspoon turmeric

½ teaspoon Dijon mustard

½ teaspoon salt

ground black pepper, to taste

100 ml/7 tablespoons crème fraîche/sour cream

50 ml/3 tablespoons mayonnaise

220–300 g/8–10½ oz. (drained weight) plain pickled Scandinavian herring

1 tablespoon chopped chives

4 boiled egg halves, to serve

SERVES 4

Peel and chop the apple into small pieces. Chop the gherkins/pickled cucumbers and capers. Add to a bowl and stir in the remaining ingredients (except the herring, chives and eggs).

Finally, add the herring pieces. Leave to marinade for a few hours in the fridge, then serve on buttered dark seeded rye bread, topped with half an egg. Garnish with chives.

CRISPY ONIONS

Many Scandinavian open sandwiches call for crispy onions. Usually, we buy them ready-made – they are just one of those useful ingredients in our cupboards. The homemade version is great and easy to make, and if you've got the time, gives your open sandwiches a nice gourmet look. Plus, homemade ones just taste better.

1 large sweet onion or
3 shallots

1 tablespoon plain/all-purpose flour

salt and freshly ground black pepper

150 ml/½ cup plus
1 tablespoon vegetable oil, for frying

**MAKES ENOUGH FOR
6-8 SANDWICHES**

If you're using shallots, cut them into rings; if you're opting for a large onion, cut it into quarters, then slice finely.

Season the flour with salt and pepper. It's easiest if you put the flour, salt and pepper into a plastic bag, add the onions and shake until the onions are all coated. Discard excess flour.

Heat the vegetable oil in a small saucepan to 130–140°C (approx. 280°F). If the temperature is too hot, the onions will burn; if it's too cold, they will be soggy.

Once the oil reaches frying temperature, add a third of the onion or 1 shallot to the oil and cook until golden brown. Remove with a slotted spoon and leave to drain on paper towels. Repeat with the other two batches.

Allow to cool slightly before using so they crisp up.

SOUSED CUCUMBER AND DILL SIDE SALAD

This quick 'salad' is great as a side to meatballs or similar dishes. It is also used as a topping on many open meat sandwiches, as well as an essential topping on the famous 'Scandi hot dog'.

60 g/⅓ cup caster/granulated sugar

100 ml/7 tablespoons white malt vinegar

100 ml/7 tablespoons water

salt and freshly ground black pepper

1 (English) cucumber

2-3 tablespoons freshly chopped dill, to taste

**MAKES ENOUGH TO
FILL 1 SMALL JAR**

In a saucepan, put the sugar, vinegar and water and bring to a simmer. When the sugar has melted, take off the heat and season generously with salt and pepper.

Thinly slice the cucumber and place in a bowl. Top with the liquid and dill, and leave for at least 30 minutes before eating. Vary the sugar to taste for a sweet or more sour salad.

This salad will keep for 4–5 days in the fridge.

FRIED PLAICE FILLETS, PRAWNS AND ASPARAGUS

Warm toppings on open sandwiches are delicious. Pan-fried plaice fillets are quick to cook and provide both a healthy and tasty lunch option. In many 'Smørrebrød' (Open Sandwich) shops in Denmark, this open sandwich is also available cold – but if you make it at home, do serve it warm, fresh from the pan: it's the best way.

butter, plus extra for frying

2 good-sized slices of dark seeded rye bread

1 egg

1 large plaice fillet, cut in half, or 2 smaller fillets

handful of dried breadcrumbs

glug of vegetable oil

TO SERVE:

mayonnaise

200 g/7 oz. prawns/shrimp

4 green asparagus spears, blanched

sprigs of dill, to garnish

salt and freshly ground black pepper

MAKES 2

Butter the bread and set aside on a serving plate.

Whisk the egg briefly with a fork. Dip each fish fillet into the egg mixture, then coat with the breadcrumbs.

Meanwhile, heat a knob/pat of butter and the oil in a frying pan/skillet until hot and quickly fry the fillets on each side until done (this will only take a few minutes – just enough to crisp up the breadcrumbs and cook the fish).

Transfer the cooked fish to the bread, dollop 1 tablespoon of mayonnaise on top, then add the prawns/shrimp and 2 spears of asparagus. Garnish with sprigs of dill and season with salt and pepper. Serve immediately.

This open sandwich is equally good served with Remoulade Sauce (see page 73) instead of mayonnaise and prawns/shrimp. That's how we eat it at my house!

SMOKED MACKEREL WITH FENNEL AND APPLE

Our friend Kobi came up with this open sandwich. We just love the crunch from the fennel and apple – it works so well with the delicious smoked mackerel. This open sandwich really does work best on dark seeded rye bread. It is one of the most popular recipes at the café – and a perfect summery open sandwich.

100 g/3½ oz. green peas, defrosted

2 teaspoons chopped chives

1 teaspoon chopped tarragon

lemon juice

drop of olive oil

salt and freshly ground black pepper

2 slices of buttered dark seeded rye bread

1 large smoked mackerel fillet

¼ fennel bulb

¼ green apple

sprigs of dill, to garnish

SERVES 2

Using a fork, crush the peas in a bowl, then add the chives and tarragon, a few drops of lemon juice, olive oil. Mix together and season with salt and pepper.

Place each slice of bread on serving plate. Add the crushed pea mixture and spread evenly.

Remove the skin from the smoked mackerel fillet and place a generous piece on top of the pea mixture (usually, around half a fillet is big enough, but this depends on personal preference).

Finely shave the fennel using a mandolin (or with a super sharp knife) and place in a bowl. Then shave the apple the same way. Combine the apple with the fennel and dress with few more drops of lemon juice, olive oil (optional) and seasoning, if needed. Spoon on top of the mackerel, garnish with dill and serve.

Note: See overleaf for the roast beef and prawn/shrimp toppings.

EGG AND PRAWN

You will be offered the classic egg and prawn open sandwich (photo on page 36) across Scandinavia. We have updated it slightly with a delicious egg salad.

butter

2 slices of dark rye bread

3 hard-boiled eggs

¼ teaspoon Dijon mustard

1 tablespoon mayonnaise

1 tablespoon chopped chives

salt and freshly ground black pepper

2–4 slices of tomato

2 small handfuls of high-quality peeled prawns/shrimp

sprigs of dill, to garnish

lemon juice

SERVES 2

Butter the bread and arrange on serving plates.

Roughly chop the eggs and mix with the mustard, mayonnaise and chives. Season to taste.

Add a few slices of tomato to the bread, then spoon the egg mixture on top. Arrange the prawns on top of the egg salad, then decorate with a sprig of dill and a squeeze of lemon.

ROAST BEEF AND CRISPY ONIONS

This is the classic Danish open sandwich (photo on page 36) and one of the most popular. You will find it on the menu at every restaurant or deli and in our homes.

butter

2 slices of dark seeded rye bread

2 green salad leaves

8 very thin slices of rare roast beef (cold) – about 60 g/2 oz. per sandwich

2 tablespoons Danish Remoulade (see page 73 or buy from speciality shops)

2 cherry tomatoes

freshly grated horseradish, to taste

1 tablespoon Crispy Onions (see page 33)

chervil sprig, to garnish

SERVES 2

Remoulade is a Danish type of piccalilli dressing that you can make yourself or buy in speciality shops. Danes like to put remoulade on a lot of foods, from beef to fish. If you cannot get hold of ready-made remoulade, there is a recipe on page 73.

Lightly butter the rye bread and arrange on serving plates.

Arrange the lettuce on the bread and then fold the roast beef neatly on top in sections. You want to try to create a bit of height to the sandwich to make it look really appetizing. This is easiest to do with very thinly sliced beef.

Next, add the remoulade dressing in the middle, cut the cherry tomatoes in half and arrange on the remoulade.

Grate the horseradish to taste and add the Crispy Onions. Garnish with a sprig of chervil.

EGG AND CREAMED COD ROE

Ask any Swede about the food they miss most from home when they're abroad and most will say 'Kalles Kaviar', a creamed cod roe sold in a tube. It may not sound exotic – but it's absolutely delicious. It is, by far, the most popular item in our shop and it is this open sandwich that is guaranteed to sell out first on the weekends...

butter

2 slices of rye bread, soft Swedish arctic bread or crispbread

salad leaves

3 boiled eggs

Kalles Kaviar

chopped chives, to taste

freshly ground black pepper

SERVES 2

I'm still to meet a Swede who doesn't like Kalles Kaviar. It must be in their genetic make up.

Butter the bread and place on serving plates. Top the bread with the salad leaves.

Using an egg slicer, slice the eggs into neat slices (or use a sharp knife), and arrange them on the salad leaves. Top with a neat serving of the Kaviar, and finally with the chives and black pepper. Serve immediately.

SUMMERY CHICKEN WITH BASIL

Basil is not a herb used much in Nordic cooking, but it goes so well here, giving the whole sandwich a lighter, fresher taste than traditional chicken with mayonnaise.

2–4 whole asparagus spears

3 tablespoons good-quality mayonnaise

½ teaspoon Dijon mustard

1 tablespoon chopped chives, plus extra to garnish

2 tablespoons chopped basil

salt and freshly ground black pepper

100 g/3½ oz. cooked chicken (leftover from the Sunday roast, or poached chicken), chopped

butter

2 slices of dark seeded rye bread

rocket/arugula leaves

SERVES 2

Blanch the asparagus in boiling water for 2 minutes, then plunge it into cold water to stop the cooking process.

Mix the mayonnaise, mustard and herbs together, season with salt and pepper.

Cut the asparagus into bite-sized pieces, then add to the dressing. Add the chicken and stir. Check the seasoning again.

Butter the bread and arrange on plates. Add the rocket/arugula leaves, then top with the chicken mixture. Finally, decorate with extra chopped chives.

This also works really well as a filling for closed sandwiches, although be sure to choose a wholesome bread with bite.

BLUE CHEESE WITH TOASTED HAZELNUTS

Blue cheese is one of life's pleasures. At the café, we also add the crushed crumbs of 'Pepparkakor' ginger biscuits on top of this open sandwich (in Sweden, blue cheese and ginger thins are often served together). Trust me, it works really well!

butter

2 slices of dark seeded rye bread

lamb's lettuce or other leaves

20 g/1 heaped tablespoon hazelnuts

120 g/4 oz. good, soft blue cheese (we love Danish Kornblomst and Blue Castello)

2 teaspoons cloudberry jam or lingonberry compote

SERVES 2

Butter the bread, then add the salad leaves.

Toast the hazelnuts in a hot frying pan/skillet for a few minutes, then remove and lightly crush.

Carefully slice the cheese (use a warm knife and slice the cheese when it is cold – it's easier). Place neatly on top of the leaves.

Add the cloudberry jam or compote on top of the cheese and top with the crushed hazelnuts.

THE SCANDI LUNCH SOLUTION

A Scandinavian open sandwich is a slice of buttered, decorated bread. Topless. For lunch at home we take a piece of bread, spread it lightly with butter, then add a tasty topping, such as smoked salmon, ham or cheese. Simple is the Nordic way. Outside Scandinavia, people tend to view open sandwiches as something fancy and fiddly – and perhaps slightly impractical. To us, it's just how we eat lunch.

In Denmark, where open sandwiches are eaten most days, even a packed lunch at school comprises open sandwiches – not the elaborate pieces of art you see in the fancy restaurants, of course, but just a piece of simple rye bread with pâté, ham or egg. But growing up, we never had white bread except on Sundays.

The beauty of the open sandwich is about how it means you eat less bread overall – and better bread, too. You top it with good-quality toppings because you simply can't hide your fillings between two slices of mass-produced bread by just adding more mayonnaise. Open sandwiches are a filling, but varied lunch, which don't leave you feeling like you've eaten a door-stopper wedge of bread.

Here at ScandiKitchen, we are well known for our open sandwiches, which we introduced as alternative lunchtime fare to London's vibrant food scene. We like variety, and always make a huge selection of over 20 different open sandwiches ready for lunch, allowing guests to pick and choose their favourites. Initially, we wondered if other people would find this way of eating lunch as appealing as we do – and, luckily, time has proven us right. Despite how busy Londoners are, they are happy to take the time to sit down, eat three open sandwiches with a knife and fork, and chat to their colleagues. And they are happy to do this on weekdays, not just weekends. It seems that we were not the only ones fed up with a pre-packaged sandwich and eating at our desks!

Nordic people eat a lot of wholegrain bread, rye seeded bread and a lot of crispbread. None of these types of bread can be eaten in abundance: they are simply too filling. As kids, we used to challenge each other who could eat two slices of unbuttered Danish rye bread in under a minute: You just can't. You'll find that further south in Denmark, the breads are more rye-based and seeded – and when you head north to Sweden and Norway, the soft bread is either sweeter or more wheat-based with a crust – or people use rye and wheat crispbread instead.

From this simple starting point in the home, open sandwiches have developed into more carefully constructed creations in cafés and restaurants, and for special occasions. The Scandinavian words for 'open sandwich' ('Smørrebrød' in Danish, 'Smørbrød' in Norwegian and 'Smörgås' in Swedish) literally translate as 'buttered bread' – a much more fitting description than 'sandwich'.

There is a knack to making an open sandwich look pretty and appetizing. In Scandinavia, we expect our fancier open sandwiches to appeal to the eye, as well as to the stomach. A visit to Copenhagen's cafés, with their intricately constructed Smørrebrød taking pride of place, demonstrates just how serious we take the art of constructing an open

The humble open sandwich is healthy, beautiful and satisfying.

sandwich. In Denmark, it's even possible to attain the professional qualification Open Sandwich Master.

We have included some of our favourite open sandwich recipes here for you to make at home – perfect for any lunch with friends. Not only do they look very pretty on the serving plate, they are also super tasty and good for you. While there are tried and tested traditional open sandwiches, do not be afraid to create your own new Nordic style 'Smørrebrød' – only your imagination sets the limits. All the recipes here are for two open sandwiches. They are larger than the café sandwiches we serve as they use whole sides of rye bread, so two open sandwiches per person is fitting for a good lunch (or three if you are really hungry). Alternatively, cut the sandwiches into four and create a larger variety for your guests – they even work well as canapés.

HAM AND WHITE ASPARAGUS

A very traditional Danish open sandwich that is quick to make. In Denmark, it is known as 'Italian Salad'.

butter

2 slices of dark seeded rye bread

small handful of green leaves

4 thick slices of cooked ham

sprig of chervil or chopped chives, to garnish

TOPPING:

2 white or green asparagus spears*

50 g/1¾ oz. carrots, cooked and cubed

50 g/¼ cup peas, defrosted

2 tablespoons mayonnaise

2 tablespoons crème fraîche or sour cream

tiny bit of Dijon mustard

dash of lemon juice

SERVES 2

Traditionally, white asparagus from a jar is used in this topping (you can get these at larger supermarkets/grocery stores), but during asparagus season, we use fresh green asparagus.

If using fresh green asparagus, blanch it in boiling water for 2 minutes, then plunge into cold water to stop the cooking process.

Butter the bread and arrange it on serving plates.

Top the bread with green leaves and arrange the ham on top.

To make the topping, combine all the ingredients together. Season well and arrange on top of the ham with the asparagus. Garnish with chervil or chives.

SWEDISH MEATBALLS AND BEETROOT

This is the classic Swedish sandwich. You can make this with store-bought Swedish meatballs, or with leftover Real Swedish Meatballs (see page 92).

butter

2 slices of seeded crusty bread

6–8 slices of drained, pickled beet(root), chopped into 1 cm/½ in. pieces

1 teaspoon mayonnaise

1 teaspoon crème fraîche or sour cream

drop of lemon juice

10–12 meatballs, sliced

gherkin/pickled cucumbers, sliced (optional)

chervil or parsley, to garnish

SERVES 2

Butter the bread and arrange on serving plates. Mix together the chopped beet(root), mayonnaise, crème fraîche or sour cream, and season with salt and pepper and a drop of lemon juice. Depending on the type of pickled beet(root), you may need to sweeten the mixture with a pinch of sugar as some brands are quite tart.

Arrange the beet(root) mixture on the bread, then add the meatballs on top. Optionally, add some gherkins/pickled cucumbers.

Garnish with a sprig of chervil or chopped parsley.

EGG AND SPRAT SALAD ('GUBBRÖRA')

Gubbröra literally means 'old guy's mix' in Swedish. The delicious pickled sprats (confusingly known as 'ansjovis' in Swedish, but quite different from regular anchovies) work so well with the egg. If you can't get hold of Swedish 'ansjovis' sprat fillets, you can use an equivalent weight of pickled herring instead. This open sandwich also makes a delicious appetizer, served on small rounds of crispbread or regular bread.

125 g/4½ oz. Swedish pickled sprat fillet (Grebbestad Ansjovis)

4 hard-boiled eggs

1 small red onion

1 tablespoon capers

2 tablespoons chopped chives

2 tablespoons chopped dill

3–4 tablespoons crème fraîche or sour cream

1 teaspoon Kalles Kaviar (Swedish caviar spread) (optional)

salt and freshly ground black pepper

2 slices of dark rye bread or crispbread

butter

sprigs of dill and chopped chives, to garnish

SERVES 2

Drain the sprats. Finely chop the eggs and red onion.

Mix all the ingredients together (except the bread, butter and garnish) to form a creamy salad. Serve on crispbread or buttered rye bread.

Garnish with sprigs of dill and chopped chives.

SEAFOOD SALAD ON SOURDOUGH TOAST ('SKAGENRÖRA')

Skagenröra is one of the most famous appetizers or light lunches in Sweden. It's a mixture of prawns/shrimp, creamy dressing and dill, served on toast. It was created by the popular Swedish restaurateur Tore Wretman and the original recipe features fried toast, but we prefer serving it on a nice toasted slice of good sourdough bread. The original recipe also only contained mayonnaise, but we feel that a lighter version using crème fraîche is really nice. We like to add grated horseradish. You can use either prawns/shrimp or a mixture of prawns/shrimp and crayfish tails.

2 large slices of sourdough bread

butter

couple of rocket/arugula leaves, to garnish

lumpfish roe red caviar (optional)

TOPPING:

50 ml/3 tablespoons mayonnaise

100 ml/7 tablespoons crème fraîche/sour cream

2 tablespoons fresh, finely chopped dill, plus extra sprigs to serve

2 tablespoons fresh finely chopped chives

1 shallot, finely chopped

¼ teaspoon grated lemon zest

¼ teaspoon fresh grated horseradish (or from a jar, but check the strength)

¼ teaspoon Dijon mustard

squeeze of lemon juice

salt and freshly ground black pepper

200 g/7 oz. good-quality fresh prawns/shrimp (or a mixture of prawns/shrimp and crayfish tails)

SERVES 2

Mix all the ingredients together for the topping, folding in the seafood carefully. Leave in the fridge for a few hours for the flavours to mingle.

To assemble, toast the bread lightly and butter. Add the rocket/arugula leaves, then add half the topping to each sandwich just before serving.

Decorate with a dill sprig and, optionally, a small tablespoon of red lumpfish roe.

Note: Skagenröra also makes a great filling for baked potatoes, or you can serve it alongside a green salad.

The perfect summer open sandwich: shellfish and creamy mayonnaise. Indulgent and delicious.

SMOKED SALMON AND EGG

2 slices of crusty white bread

butter

pea shoots or lamb's lettuce (optional)

2 boiled eggs

100–150 g/3½–5½ oz. good-quality smoked salmon

2 slices of lemon

6 slices of (English) cucumber

sprigs of dill

DILL SAUCE:

2 tablespoons crème fraîche/sour cream

1 tablespoon cream cheese

1 tablespoon chopped dill

1 teaspoon lemon zest

a few drops of lemon juice

¼ teaspoon grated horseradish

salt and ground black pepper

SERVES 2

Smoked salmon is by far the most popular topping on our open sandwiches at the café. What's not to love? A great slice of bread topped with beautifully smoked fish is such a simple thing, but so very tasty.

Butter the bread and arrange the pea shoots or salad leaves, if using, on each slice.

Slice the eggs and arrange on one side of the bread, then arrange the smoked salmon on the rest of the bread, slightly overlapping.

Mix the dressing and add a large tablespoon on top of the salmon, decorate with the lemon and cucumber slices and finally add a few sprigs of dill.

NEW POTATOES, AIOLI AND CRISPY ONIONS

Danes love cold, sliced potato on their open sandwiches – when the new potatoes start appearing on the market, this is one of the most delicious open sandwiches to make at home. It's also a good way to use leftover potatoes from yesterday's dinner.

butter

2 slices of dark seeded rye bread

rocket/arugula leaves

4–5 cooked, cooled new potatoes

2 tablespoons aïoli

3 tablespoons Crispy Onions (see page 33)

1 tablespoon chopped chives

thinly sliced red onion rings (optional)

salt and ground black pepper

SERVES 2

Butter the bread and arrange on two serving plates.

Scatter the base of the bread with the rocket/arugula leaves.

Slice the potatoes and place neatly on the bread.

Add a good tablespoon of aïoli to each sandwich, then add the fried crispy onion and finish with a scattering of chives. Add a few red onion rings, if preferred. Season to taste.

Early morning mists on the lake.
We call this fog 'älvdans', which
translates as 'elves dancing'.

SALADS, SOUPS AND LIGHTER DISHES

Our homemade seasonal salads are hugely popular at the café and we make so many different kinds throughout the year that it was hard to narrow down to just a few for this book. We ended up asking our team and customers for their favourites. For the days when you want something a little bit lighter for lunch or dinner – or just fancy adding new extra side dishes to your Smörgåsbord.

SWEET POTATO SALAD WITH TARRAGON AND RYE .

Our friend Kobi Ruzicka came up with this salad and it has been a bestseller at the café. I think it perfectly marries the bite of the grain with the sweetness of the potatoes and the sharpness of the onion and tarragon. Although not a traditional Scandinavian salad, it has all the flavours of one. Serve slightly warm or cold.

100 g/3½ oz. dry rye grains

salt and freshly ground black pepper

4–6 sweet potatoes (depending on size)

olive oil

1 bunch fresh tarragon

1 bunch spring onions/ scallions, outer layer removed and sliced diagonally

200 g/7 oz. feta cheese

balsamic vinegar

SERVES 2–3

If soaking the grains overnight (I'd recommend this if you have time as it allows for a more even texture throughout), place them in double the amount of water.

The next day, drain and rinse the grains. Place in a large saucepan with a good pinch of salt and boil for approximately 20–22 minutes, or until tender. If you haven't pre-soaked the grains, cook for around 40 minutes. Drain and allow to cool completely.

Preheat the oven to 160°C (320°F) Gas 3.

Wash and cut the sweet potatoes into bite- sized pieces (leave the skin on), and toss with oil, salt and pepper. Place on a baking sheet and roast in the preheated oven, turning occasionally, for around 20 minutes or until cooked through.

Separate the leaves of the tarragon from the stalks (which you can discard) and place in a large serving bowl. Add the spring onions/ scallions. With your fingers, lightly crumble the feta into the same bowl and set aside.

When the sweet potato is cooked, remove from oven and allow to cool slightly, then add to a serving bowl. Add the cooled rye grains and fold everything together carefully so as not to break up the potatoes. Adjust the seasoning, and add more olive oil and a dash of balsamic vinegar, if needed.

Tips: Cooked grains keep for a few days in the fridge and can be made ahead. You can easily make this salad with spelt grain or other grains instead of rye, but adjust the cooking time accordingly.

ARTICHOKE SALAD WITH SPELT GRAINS

It's no secret that we love using grains in our salads at ScandiKitchen. Spelt is such a filling, wholesome grain – and it has an excellent bite to it. If you are not a fan of spelt, you can use rye grains instead.

150 g/1 cup dried spelt grains

salt and freshly ground black pepper

2 x 250 g/9 oz. cans of artichoke hearts, drained

150 g/5½ oz. feta cheese, chopped into cubes

½ bunch spring onions/ scallions, sliced diagonally

2 tablespoons chopped fresh flat-leaf parsley

4–5 tablespoons flaked/ slivered almonds, toasted

freshly squeezed lemon juice

olive oil, for drizzling

SERVES 2-3
AS A SIDE SALAD

If soaking the grains overnight (I'd recommend this if you have time as it allows for a more even texture throughout), place them in double the amount of water.

The next day, drain and rinse the grains. Place in a large saucepan with a good pinch of salt and boil for approximately 22–25 minutes, or until tender but still al dente. If you haven't pre-soaked the grains, extend the cooking time by around 20 minutes. Drain and allow to cool completely.

Slice the artichoke hearts into large bite-sized pieces. Place in a bowl and add the sliced spring onions/scallions, feta and parsley.

Fold in the spelt grains, season to taste and fold in the toasted almond flakes.

Season with salt, pepper and a squeeze of lemon juice and a drizzle of good oil.

A fresh, tangy salad; replace the spelt with any of your favourite grains – try rye or wheatberry for variation.

GRAVLAX AND NEW POTATO SALAD

We often make this salad at the café if we have some 'gravlax' cured salmon left over. Simple cold new potatoes and cured salmon is such a delicious combination. You can mix and match whatever vegetables you prefer into this salad – use the list below as a guideline. You can even omit the potatoes if you want the dish less carb-heavy (I usually add a few wedges of boiled eggs when I omit the potatoes). The dressing for this salad is simply the normal Gravlax sauce (recipe below), used to dress traditional cured salmon.

300 g/10½ oz. cooked, cooled new potatoes, halved, or sliced if preferred

200 g/7 oz. cured salmon (or normal smoked salmon)

100 g/3½ oz. green beans, blanched lightly, cooled and cut into 3–4-cm/1–1½-in. pieces

150 g/5½ oz. green asparagus, blanched lightly, cooled and cut into 3–4-cm/1–1½-in. pieces

100 g/3½ oz. peas, blanched and cooled

10 cherry tomatoes, halved

⅓ cucumber, cubed into bite-sized pieces

large handful of crunchy green salad leaves

1 tablespoon fresh chopped chives

sprigs of dill, to decorate

GRAVLAX SAUCE:

2 tablespoons Swedish Mustard (we really like using Slotts Senap – but if you can't get Swedish, go for a good grainy Dijon; however, you may need to add extra sugar)

4 tablespoons finely chopped fresh dill

1 tablespoon white wine vinegar

1 teaspoon sugar

pinch of salt and ground black pepper

100 ml/7 tablespoons rapeseed/canola oil

SERVES 3–4

For the gravlax sauce, mix the mustard, dill, vinegar, sugar and salt and pepper in a bowl. Add the oil carefully, start by adding a few drops, then steadily adding a thin stream of oil to emulsify the dressing as you continue to whisk. If you add it too quickly it will split. Keep whisking until you have a good, creamy consistency. Add a little bit more oil if it is too thick.

Fold together all the ingredients, dress lightly with Gravlax Sauce and sprigs of dill and serve.

KALE, RED GRAPE, HAZELNUT AND VÄSTERBOTTEN CHEESE SALAD

This is a super easy and delicious salad. Västerbotten is an aged Swedish cheese, revered as the King of Swedish cheeses. It has a firm but crumbly texture with a good, strong bite to it. Many speciality shops stock this versatile cheese, which you can slice and serve on bread, use in cooking and add to salads. According to legend, Västerbotten cheese was created by accident when cheesemaker Ulrika Eleonora Lindström was left alone to stir the curd of a traditional Swedish cheese, but was 'distracted' on several occasions by visits from her lover. The fire went out on the stove and the curds cooled several times. As a result of this, the cheese didn't meet the grade and was set aside for a year. When it was finally tasted, the cheesemakers realised they'd made something significant and utterly delicious. If you cannot get hold of Västerbotten, use Pecorino instead.

small bunch of kale (about 200 g/7 oz.)

1–2 tablespoons lemon juice

1–2 tablespoons good-quality olive oil

salt and freshly ground black pepper

1 large tablespoon roughly chopped, toasted hazelnuts

about 25 red grapes

40 g/1½ oz. Västerbotten or Pecorino cheese shavings

SERVES 2 AS A SIDE SALAD

Discard the stems of the kale and chop the leaves. Add the lemon juice, oil, salt and pepper to the kale and gently massage the leaves until they tenderize. This takes a few minutes and you will see the kale go a darker green colour (massaging makes the kale's tough cellulose structure break down and wilt a bit). Taste it: if it is no longer bitter, it's done.

Add the toasted hazelnuts to the salad along with the halved red grapes and Västerbotten cheese shavings. Serve immediately.

APPLE, BROCCOLI, KALE AND RYE SALAD

We love kale mixed with sweet apple – it's just such a fresh combination.

100 g/½ cup rye grains

200 g /7 oz. tenderstem broccoli/broccolini

80 g/2 cups kale

freshly squeezed lemon juice

1 red sweet apple

olive oil

raspberry vinegar

salt and freshly ground black pepper

50 g/½ cup plus 1 tablespoon hazelnuts, toasted in the oven for 5 minutes

SERVES 3–4 AS A SIDE

Soak the rye grains overnight in double the amount of water. Alternatively, you'll need to cook the grains for longer. Drain and rinse the soaked grains. Place in a large saucepan with a good pinch of salt and boil for around 25 minutes if soaked, and 40 minutes if not, or until al-dente. Drain and allow to cool completely.

Boil the broccoli for 2–3 minutes. Drain and leave to cool down in very cold water to stop the cooking process. Cut into small pieces.

Pick the kale off the stems and slice into thin strips. Massage very gently using your hands in a bowl with a bit of lemon juice until it changes colour to dark green and becomes soft.

Chop the apple into bite-sized pieces and toss in lemon juice to prevent discoloring. Mix all the ingredients (except nuts) together in a bowl and season with salt and pepper and a glug of good olive oil and a drizzle of raspberry vinegar. Crush the nuts slightly and scatter on top of the salad just before serving.

TRADITIONAL APPLE AND BEETROOT SALAD

A staple on any Scandinavian Smörgåsbord, pickled beet(root) and apple salad can be enjoyed on its own or with meatballs – or even as part of a larger salad.

approx. 280 g/10 oz. pickled beet(root), cut into 1-cm/½-in. pieces

½ Granny Smith apple (or similar tart apple), cut into 1-cm/½-in. pieces

50 g/3 tablespoons mayonnaise

50 g/3 tablespoons crème fraîche/sour cream

squeeze of lemon juice

dash of balsamic vinegar

salt and freshly ground black pepper

1 tablespoon chopped chives (optional)

SERVES 4 AS A SIDE

Mix the beet(root) and apple in a bowl, add the mayonnaise, crème fraîche/sour cream, lemon juice and balsamic vinegar and stir. You are looking for a good creamy consistency and a medium pink colour (if the beet(root) is not drained properly, you will get a runny consistency). Season to taste (add sugar if using a tart variety of pickled beet(root)). Add more mayonnaise and crème fraîche/sour cream if a creamier salad is desired.

Leave to set in the fridge for a few hours or even overnight. If it goes too dark, add a bit more crème fraîche/sour cream or mayonnaise just before serving. If using chives, add chopped on top before serving.

For the Christmas Smörgåsbord, my father-in-law Leif adds a handful of finely chopped 'Smörgåsgurka' gherkins and folds in a spoonful of whipped cream at the end to make it extra creamy. Well, there are no calories in Christmas food, as we all know...

SMØRREBRØ

SMÖRGÅSBORD

'Smörgåsbord' comes from the Swedish words 'smörgås' meaning 'open sandwich' or 'buttered bread' and 'bord', meaning 'table'. Translated, it basically means a buffet made up of many smaller dishes. It's not to be confused with the Danish word 'Smørrebrød', which just means 'open sandwich'.

The term Smörgåsbord first cropped up in English during the World Fair in New York in 1939, where a Swedish restaurant served Smörgåsbord as it is known today. However, the tradition actually started several hundred years earlier when it was known as 'Aquavit Table'. A few hours prior to dinner, shots of aquavit were served, accompanied by a selection of cheeses, pickles and meats laid out on a side table to snack on before going for the main meal. Over the years, the choice of dishes expanded. Eventually, everything moved onto the main dinner table and thus 'Smörgåsbord' was born, in the mid-17th century.

The traditional Smörgåsbord has a different twist depending on the country you are in. However, whether you're in Denmark, Sweden or Norway, we eat our Smörgåsbord in a certain order, known as 'rounds'. This comprises: Round 1: pickled herring and ice-cold aquavit; Round 2: fish and seafood dishes; Round 3: cold meats and pies; Round 4: warm meats; Round 5: cheese selection; and Round 6: dessert (and coffee). In Sweden and Norway, all the dishes are laid out at the beginning, but you only vaguely adhere to the 'order', although less so at casual family gatherings than with Smorgasbord gatherings at formal restaurants. In Denmark, the dishes are mostly served at the main table, and brought out one after the other.

The food on the table is not cleared away until the very end, except for the herring.

Smörgåsbord encourages conversation and chit-chatting. It's about taking the time to eat very slowly, taking small bites and eating small portions, and being able to fit in a bit of every course. The hardest thing for Smörgåsbord novices is getting used to pacing themselves as the food starts arriving – a little goes a long way. A rookie can be spotted during the first 'round', helping themselves to several slices of bread and half the pot of herring, and thinking the aquavit won't have much effect.

Today, the biggest Smörgåsbord of the year is at Christmas time, when it's called 'Julbord' ('Christmas Table'). The event can easily take anything from 5–6 hours to complete. During this time, you will work your way through all the different 'rounds', as well as a considerable amount of both beer and aquavit. There may be singing (some families are more inclined than others – in mine, we sing from start to finish). People in Scandinavia attend many Julbord lunches throughout December (at work or with friends), but the biggest one is always on Christmas Eve with the family.

We also have 'Smörgåsbord' at Easter, midsummer and birthdays. When growing up in my family's house, my mother always made a Friday evening Smörgåsbord, where she added any leftovers from the week in little dishes as well as pickled herring, smoked fish and bread. It quickly became a wonderful family tradition for Friday evenings where we would stay up late, eating and catching up about the week. I carry on this tradition today in our own house in London!

By the end of our Friday-night Smörgåsbord, we've solved the world's problems and planned our week ahead.

NORDIC FISH SOUP

We love fish in Scandinavia – especially in soups – and there are many different family recipes and regional versions of fish soup. This is a simple and hearty dish that you can adapt with whatever fish and seafood you like. Liven it up with the herbs of your choice – dill or chives work well if you prefer a fresher flavour.

1.25–1.5 litres/6–7 cups high-quality fish stock

2–3 shallots

1 celery stick, finely chopped

1 leek (discard the green section at the top), sliced

1 large carrot, finely chopped

1 parsnip, finely chopped

good handful of fresh clams (about 300 g/10½ oz. weight, including shells) or ready-cooked clams

25 g/2 tablespoons butter

1 onion, chopped

25 g/2 tablespoons plain/all-purpose flour

salt and freshly ground black pepper

dash of white wine vinegar

150 ml/⅔ cup double/heavy cream

lemon juice (optional)

pinch of sugar (optional)

300–400 g/10½–14 oz. cod, haddock and pollock fillet, skin removed

150–200 g/5½–7 oz. raw large prawns/jumbo shrimp

crusty bread, to serve

SERVES 4 AS A MAIN OR 6 AS A STARTER

Bring 500 ml/2 cups of the stock to the boil in a saucepan. Add the vegetables. Leave to simmer on a low heat, covered, until the vegetables are cooked (about 7–10 minutes, depending on the size of the pieces). Set aside (don't discard the the stock).

If you are using fresh clams, steam and open these separately. Firstly, ensure they are scrubbed clean, then steam them over an inch of water until the shells open. Take off the heat and set aside (ensure you discard any that have not opened during cooking). If using ready-cooked clams, you do not need to do this: you can add them directly to soup at the end.

Add the butter to a large saucepan and gently cook the onion, taking care not to colour it. Add the flour and stir. Once incorporated, start adding the remaining stock slowly, bringing to the boil continuously to make a sauce. Keep adding the stock until it's all used, then add the vegetable and stock mixture. If the soup is too thick, add some water to reach a light soup consistency. Leave to simmer for 5–7 minutes.

Season with salt and pepper and a dash of white wine vinegar. Turn off the heat, add the cream and stir through. If needed, add a few drops of lemon juice, to taste. If the soup is too sharp, I often add a pinch of sugar.

Cut your fish into small pieces and add raw to the soup (it will cook in about 5 minutes in the hot liquid). Turn off the heat. Add the prawns/shrimp. Lastly, add the clams in their shells and serve immediately with crusty bread.

BRISKET OF BEEF SOUP WITH DUMPLINGS

This is the ultimate hearty Danish soup. It reminds most Danes of dark autumn evenings, warm soup and mother's cosy kitchen. Serve with a wedge of crusty bread.

1–1½ kg/2¼–3¼ lbs. beef brisket

3 celery sticks

3 carrots

1 large onion

3 leeks

2 parsnips

10 peppercorns

2 bay leaves

salt

MEATBALLS (MAKES 40):

350 g/12½ oz. minced/ground beef and pork (half and half), or just beef, if you prefer

1 egg

2 tablespoons breadcrumbs

1 tablespoon grated onion

150 ml/⅔ cup milk

salt and freshly ground black pepper

DUMPLINGS (MAKES 30–40):

200 ml/¾ cup water

75 g/5 tablespoons butter

100 g/¾ cup plain/all-purpose flour

2 eggs

1 teaspoon salt

SERVES 4

To make the soup, cover the brisket with water in a stock pot. Bring to the boil and skim the froth off the top as best you can. Add half of the vegetables, all the peppercorns and bay leaves and a good helping of salt. Leave to simmer for 3 hours (ensure the meat is well covered by liquid). Remove the meat from the pot and set aside (see tip below). Pour the contents of the soup through a sieve/strainer, discard the cooked vegetables and return the soup to the pot. If you have a muslin/cheesecloth, strain the soup through it to remove impurities. Cube the remaining vegetables, slice the leek and add to the pot. Simmer for 10 minutes, adjust the seasoning and it's ready.

To make the meatballs, add all the ingredients to a food processor and mix well. Leave to set for about 30 minutes before using. Heat a pot of water to boiling point. Put the meat mixture into a piping bag with a 1-cm/½-in. opening and press out the meatballs, cutting the meat off with scissors directly into the simmering water to cook for 3–4 minutes. You can roll them by hand but this will take quite some time. Remove the cooked meatballs with a slotted spoon and set aside.

For the dumplings, add the water to a saucepan with the butter and bring to the boil. Whisk in the flour, then add the eggs one at the time. Use a spatula as the mixture gets smoother and thicker. Add salt and pepper and take off the heat once the mixture no longer sticks to the side of the pan (a few minutes).

Heat a saucepan of water and keep just below simmering. Transfer the flour mixture to a piping bag and pipe out individual dumplings through a piping bag with a 1-cm/½-in. opening, using scissors to cut each dumpling from the piping bag directly into the saucepan. Leave to cook for a few minutes until the dumplings rise to the surface. Remove with a slotted spoon and set aside.

To serve, add the meatballs to the soup and heat to boiling point, then take off the heat. Add the dumplings and leave to heat for a few minutes.

Tip: To use the cooked brisket in a different dish, reserve 400 ml/1⅔ cups of the clear soup, make a roux of butter and flour and add the soup to make a sauce. Add 80 ml/⅓ cup of single/light cream, freshly grated horseradish, salt and pepper and a dash of white wine vinegar. Serve with boiled potatoes and slices of beef.

NORDIC FISH CAKES WITH DANISH REMOULADE

Super-quick and easy fish cakes – a perfect addition to your Smörgåsbord. Danish remoulade dressing differs from the traditional French version – we flavour it with curry powder and use it on pretty much anything – from fish to cold roast beef.

400 g/14 oz. cod loin, haddock, pollock or similar

1 teaspoon flaked salt

1 floury potato

50 ml/3 tablespoons single/light cream

120 ml/½ cup whole milk

1 egg

1½ tablespoons chopped dill

1½ tablespoons chopped chives

1 tablespoon plain/all-purpose flour

salt and ground black pepper

butter, for frying

DANISH REMOULADE:

50 g/2 oz. carrot, finely chopped

50 g/2 oz. cauliflower, finely chopped

25 g/1 oz. white cabbage, finely chopped

25 g/1 oz. gherkins/pickled cucumbers, finely chopped

1 tablespoon capers

1 tablespoon chopped shallot

1 teaspoon chopped chives

150 ml/⅔ cup good-quality mayonnaise

100 ml/7 tablespoons crème fraîche/sour cream

½ teaspoon curry powder

1 teaspoon turmeric (optional)

1 teaspoon coarse mustard

1 teaspoon white wine vinegar

1 teaspoon lemon juice

2 tablespoons icing/confectioners' sugar (to taste)

salt and ground black pepper

MAKES 10

In a food processor, add the fish and salt and pulse until blended.

Grate the potato finely and squeeze out the excess liquid. Add the potato to a bowl along with the remaining ingredients. Mix well and add to the food processor. Blend until well combined. Transfer the mixture to the fridge for 30 minutes before using.

Meanwhile, make the Remoulade (see Note below): mix all the ingredients together until well combined. For quick results, pulse a few times in a food processor or with a stick blender. Leave in the fridge for 30 minutes before using to allow the colour and flavour to develop. Note that this makes quite a large amount of dressing, but it will keep in fridge for up to 5 days. Store-bought remoulade is very sweet – if you're used to this taste, you can add more sugar to the final result to match the store-bought versions.

Heat up a large frying pan/skillet and add a good knob/pat of butter. Using a tablespoon and the palm of your hand, shape egg-sized balls and add to the butter. Squash the fish cakes down gently to give them slightly flatter surfaces. Fry until golden brown and crisp on both sides (3–4 minutes per side). Keep warm in an oven on a low temperature while you fry the remaining fish cakes.

Enjoy warm with a dollop of remoulade and slices of buttered rye bread. These fish cakes are also excellent cold as an open sandwich filling.

Note: To Scandinavians, remoulade is a yellow curried dressing (in contrast to original French remoulade which bears little resemblance to our Scandi version). It's especially popular in Denmark, where it's enjoyed with almost anything. Most people buy it ready-made in food stores, but making it at home is much more wholesome.

BEETROOT TART WITH FENNEL AND DILL

I just love the purple beet(root) with the fresh green dill – it brightens up the whole lunch table. The tart works well both warm and cold and it is lighter than traditional quiches as it uses less dairy filling.

3–4 fresh beet(root), approx. 300 g/10½ oz. raw weight; alternatively, you can use 1 x 250 g/9 oz. pack of ready-cooked beet(root)

200 ml/¾ cup plus 1 tablespoon crème fraîche/ sour cream

100 ml/7 tablespoons milk

2 eggs

200 g/7 oz. feta cheese, crumbled

salt and freshly ground black pepper

1 tablespoon fresh dill

1 fennel bulb

olive oil

balsamic vinegar

50 g/⅔ cup walnuts, lightly crushed

PASTRY:

150 g/1 stick plus 2 tablespoons butter

150 g/1 cup plus 1 tablespoon plain/all-purpose flour

100 g/1 scant cup wholegrain rye flour

pinch of salt

1 egg yolk

4 tablespoons cold water

fluted, loose-based round pie tin, approx. 28 cm/11 in. diameter

SERVES 6–7

If using fresh beet(root), put them in a large saucepan of water and bring to the boil. Cook for 30–40 minutes (depending on the size of the beet(root) until soft. Rinse in cold water. The peel will come off easily when you rub them with your fingers. Set aside.

To make the pastry, cube the butter and crumble it with the flours and salt. This is quickly done in a food processor. Add the egg yolk and water and quickly, without working the dough too much, shape into a ball. Leave to chill in the fridge or freezer for 30 minutes before using.

Roll out the dough and carefully place into the fluted loose-based pie tin. Prick the bottom of the case with a fork in several places. Leave to rest for another 15 minutes in the fridge or freezer.

Preheat the oven to 180°C (350°F) Gas 4.

Pre-bake the crust in the middle of the preheated oven for around 10 minutes.

Meanwhile, mix the crème fraîche/sour cream, milk, eggs, crumbled feta, salt, pepper and half the dill in a bowl.

Cut the fennel lengthways and remove the bottom core. Thinly slice the fennel. In a saucepan, add a little oil and sauté the fennel on a low heat for 5–6 minutes. After a few minutes, add a few teaspoons of balsamic vinegar.

Remove the crust from the oven. Scatter the sautéed fennel across the base and add one-third of the crème fraîche/sour cream mixture. Thinly slice the beet(root) and arrange the thin slices all across the tart in neat layers. Add the remaining crème fraîche/sour cream dressing on top and scatter with half of the crushed walnuts.

Return to the middle of the oven for around 20–25 minutes. When done, scatter the remaining dill and walnuts on top. Serve warm.

Cycling is one of the nicest and
most beautiful ways to explore
the Scandinavian countryside.

THIS PAGE: Hasselback Potatoes   OPPOSITE: Danish Roast Pork (Flæskesteg)

DINNER

Scandinavians are simple folk. We eat from the land and sea, we work hard, and our home dinner traditions reflect this. We don't 'do' fancy; we do hearty. We do good produce, simply prepared. Of course, you can go out and eat expertly prepared New Nordic food made from foraged ingredients harvested by maidens in the moonlight – but this is not what you will find in our kitchens at home. Here, you will find good food made with a lot of love and tradition that will fill your belly.

PORK, PICKLED BEETROOT AND POTATO HASH (PYTTIPANNA)

In Swedish and Norwegian, this dish translates as 'pieces in the pan'. In Denmark, the same dish is called 'Biksemad' and means 'mixed food'. It is a great way to use leftover meat from the Sunday roast. What makes it Nordic is the essential addition of pickled beet(root) and fried eggs, giving the dish a good sharpness as well as an instant sauce from the runny egg yolk. We eat this for lunch or dinner. This dish only works if the potatoes are firm so they can be cubed and fried – mushy leftover roasties will not work well for this. Pytt Bellmann is a Swedish variation of Pyttipanna. It's always made with chopped veal or beef, and a dash of cream is added at the end to make a creamier dish.

500 g/1 lb. 2 oz. cold, cooked potatoes

300 g/10½ oz. cooked meat leftovers – roast pork or beef or a mixture of the two

200 g/7 oz. onion

75 g/2½ oz. bacon lardons or back bacon, cut into small rectangular pieces

25 g/2 tablespoons butter

olive oil

salt and freshly ground black pepper

1 tablespoon chopped flat-leaf parsley

4–8 eggs

Worcestershire sauce

green beans, blanched

pickled beet(root), sliced

SERVES 4

Cut the potatoes and meat into similar-sized pieces (about 1 cm/½ in.)

Chop the onion and bacon (unless you're using lardons) and set aside.

In a deep ovenproof frying pan/skillet, melt the butter and a drop of olive oil. Heat up, then add the potatoes and fry until they are golden and have crisped up.

Remove the potatoes from the pan/skillet, add a bit more oil (if needed), then add the onion and bacon and cook until done. Add the meat, heat through, and carefully fold in the potatoes again (the reason you cook and add the potatoes in two actions is to ensure they keep their shape and do not turn the dish to mush).

Season with salt and pepper and parsley and transfer to a low oven to keep warm.

Meanwhile, fry the eggs in another frying pan/skillet. If your guests are a hungry sort, cook two fried eggs per person. If not, fry one each. Serve each portion of Pyttipanna topped with the fried egg(s), a few drops of Worcestershire sauce to taste, a few blanched green beans and sliced beet(root). Some people add ketchup, too.

FISH GRATIN (FISKGRATÄNG)

I grew up in the 1980s and embrace everything from A-ha to Joey Tempest, mullet hairstyles and fish bakes with piped mashed potato on top. This sort of dish reminds many of us of midweek dinners at home when we were growing up – fish pie made from local fish, seasonal vegetables and good, hearty mash. In Sweden, the middle bit of the fish bake is traditionally left open and prawns/shrimp are added at the last minute. If you don't have a fancy piping bag, you can pipe the mash through a normal freezer bag with the corner snipped off.

4 haddock fillets (or other white fish fillets), approx. 650–700 g/1½ lbs.)

MASH:

800 g/1¾ lbs. floury potatoes

50 g/3 tablespoons butter

3 tablespoons vegetable oil

2 egg yolks

¼ teaspoon sweet mustard
salt and freshly ground black pepper

nutmeg

SAUCE:

100 g/3½ oz. green asparagus

25 g/2 tablespoons butter

25 g/2 tablespoons plain/all-purpose flour

100 ml/7 tablespoons white wine

400–500 ml/1⅔–2 cups fish stock

100 ml/7 tablespoons double/heavy cream

salt and ground black pepper

freshly squeezed lemon juice

1 egg yolk

150 g/5½ oz shell-on large prawns/jumbo shrimp, cooked

150 g/5½ oz. peeled prawns/shrimp

dill sprigs, to garnish

piping bag with star nozzle/tip

SERVES 4

First prepare the mash. Peel the potatoes and cut them into small pieces, then boil until soft. Mash, together with the butter, oil and egg yolk until completely smooth. Season with mustard, salt, pepper and a bit of nutmeg. Set aside.

Preheat the oven to 180°C (350°F) Gas 4.

In an ovenproof dish, place the fish and cover it with foil. Pop it in the preheated oven to cook for 10–12 minutes. Bear in mind that smaller pieces of fish will need less cooking; it's better to undercook slightly rather than overcook at this stage.

Meanwhile, make the sauce. Bring some water to the boil and quickly blanch the green asparagus for 1 minute before cooling in cold water. Set aside. Melt the butter in a saucepan, add the flour and whisk. Add the white wine and start adding the fish stock bit by bit to thicken the sauce, while you continue to cook. Keep whisking and adding stock until you have a nice thick sauce. Add the double/heavy cream, turn off the heat and season with salt, pepper and some lemon juice, if needed. Add the egg yolk and stir. Cut the asparagus into bite-sized pieces and add to the sauce.

Remove the cooked fish from the oven. If you are making one big pie, simply leave the fish in the dish (but drain the excess water off). If you're making individual dishes, carefully add the fish to your 4 serving dishes. Pour the thick sauce over the fish.

Spoon the potato into a piping bag and press out nice duchesse patterns all along the side of the dish, leaving the middle of the gratin open.

Pop the dish back into the oven on a high heat or grill to give the potato some colour. Add the peeled prawns/shrimp, then the whole prawns/jumbo shrimp and cook for 2 more minutes in the oven. Garnish with a few sprigs of dill and serve immediately.

JANSSON'S TEMPTATION

This is one of the most famous dishes in Sweden – and considering it's only really a side dish, that says something. It's truly delicious and unlike other potato gratins. The flavour of the dish comes from the 'Ansjovis', which are pickled sprats (and not to be confused with anchovies). Serve as part of a traditional Swedish Smörgåsbord or with roast lamb.

700 g/1½ lbs. potatoes such as King Edward or similar

25 g/2 tablespoons butter

200 g/7 oz. onion, finely sliced

1 x 125-g/4½-oz. tin of Grebbestads Ansjovis (pickled sprats in brine) or small pickled herrings

salt and freshly ground black pepper

300 ml/1¼ cups double/heavy cream

300 ml/1¼ cups whole milk

2 tablespoons dried breadcrumbs

30 x 20 cm/12 x 8 in. baking dish

SERVES 4-6 AS A SIDE

Preheat the oven to 200°C (400°F) Gas 6.

Peel the potatoes and chop them into small 0.5-cm/¼-in. piece sticks (a bit thinner than French fries). Put them on a baking sheet and place in the preheated oven for 20 minutes to pre-cook them.

Melt the butter in a saucepan, add the onion and cook until soft. Take care not to burn the onion - it should be cooked, but shouldn't turn brown.

Add the pre-cooked potatoes to the onion mixture and fold together. Layer half of the onion and potato mixture in the bottom of an ovenproof dish, then top with half the sprat fillets placed at even intervals. Season with salt and pepper and pour over half the cream and milk.

Add another layer of onion and potato, then the remaining sprats on top. Pour the remaining sprat brine, then the remaining milk and cream over the dish. Sprinkle the breadcrumbs on top and season.

Bake for about 45 minutes in the preheated oven, or until the potatoes are cooked. If the dish is looking dry, you can add more milk - the aim is to get a creamy consistency.

BAKED HALIBUT WITH MUSTARD SAUCE

This dish is simple, but super tasty. The fish bakes while you make the sauce and the whole dish is ready in a flash. Serve it with whichever healthy greens you like on a bed of wilted spinach. While halibut is an expensive fish, I think it's worth it, but you can always choose to substitute it with haddock or cod loin for a more cost-effective weekday meal.

700–800 g/1½–1¾ lbs. halibut steaks (4 pieces)

500 g/1 lb. 2 oz. spinach leaves

oil, for frying

2 shallots, finely chopped

SAUCE:

25 g/2 tablespoons butter

25 g/2 tablespoons plain/all-purpose flour

400–500 ml/1⅔–2 cups fish stock

salt and freshly ground black pepper

2 tablespoons coarse, sweet mustard

drop of white wine vinegar or drop of lemon juice (optional)

seasonal green vegetables, to serve

SERVES 4

Preheat the oven to 175°C (350°F) Gas 5

Put the fish in an ovenproof dish, season lightly and cover with foil. Bake for 10–12 minutes or until done (taking care not to overcook, so keep an eye on it – and cooking time will vary depending on the thickness of your fish steaks).

Rinse the spinach and leave to drip-dry in a colander.

Meanwhile, in a saucepan, melt the butter and add the flour to make a roux. Slowly add the fish stock as you boil it into a sauce. If you prefer a creamier sauce, you can use half milk and half stock.

Once you have a good thin sauce consistency, season with salt and pepper and then add the mustard. Do not boil the sauce after the mustard has been added. Taste again – depending on your mustard, you may need to adjust the seasoning with white wine vinegar (or lemon juice) or more salt and pepper.

Add a glug of oil to a frying pan/skillet and fry the shallots until soft, then add the spinach and wilt lightly (don't overcook it). Season with salt and pepper.

Arrange the spinach on 4 plates, add the fish and top with the sauce. Serve with seasonal green vegetables and bread. For a heartier meal, I sometimes serve a side of roasted new potatoes.

BEEF LINDSTRÖM

This famous Swedish bun-less burger is named after Henrik Lindström, a prominent Swedish industrialist who grew up in St. Petersburg with his Swedish parents. On his visits to Sweden, he taught the chef at his hotel how to make this burger with capers and beet(root) and it became a hit across the country. And rightly so: beet(root) in a burger is utterly delicious. Serve with any type of potato that you like – although at home, I love serving it with cubed, crispy fried potatoes and seasonal vegetables.

500 g/1 lb. 2 oz. minced/ground beef

salt

1 onion

100 g/3^1/$_2$ oz. pickled beet(root)

40 g/1^1/$_2$ oz. gherkins/pickled cucumbers

2 tablespoons capers

4 egg yolks

1 cooked potato (80 g/3 oz.)

1 teaspoon Dijon mustard

glug of vegetable oil, for frying

knob/pat of butter, for frying

4 eggs, for frying

salt and freshly ground black pepper

pan-fried potatoes, to serve

seasonal green vegetables, to serve

MAKES 4

In a food processor, mix the beef and salt for a short while to combine.

Finely chop the onion, beet(root) and gherkins/pickled cucumbers, and roughly chop the capers. Add these ingredients to the food processor along with the egg yolks, potato and mustard, and continue to blitz until everything is incorporated (but not too long or the burger will become too firm). Make 4 burgers and leave them to rest for 30 minutes before frying.

Add the oil and butter to a frying pan/skillet, and fry each burger on a high heat for about 3–4 minutes on each side (depending on how you prefer your burger).

Once cooked, pop the beef patties in the oven to keep warm and fry 4 eggs in your frying pan/skillet.

Serve each beef patty with an egg on top, alongside the pan-fried potatoes and seasonal green vegetables.

AUTUMN CRAYFISH FESTIVAL

Across Sweden and Finland, the crayfish season is a huge event each autumn.

Crayfish has been eaten for centuries, but fishing restrictions were imposed in the early 1900s due to the risk of overfishing. For years, people were only allowed to catch crayfish around August, creating a whole season for over-indulging.

Nowadays, fishing restrictions have been lifted, but we Scandinavians do love good old traditions, so we tend to stick to eating our crayfish from the end of July until early September. The start of the crayfish season is still a huge thing each year. Newspapers and magazines compare the season's available crayfish (now mostly imported from Turkey and China and sold ready-to-eat, to cope with the huge demand). Of course, locally caught crayfish will always win, but it is also in the shortest supply and the most expensive. When a Swede hosts a crayfish party, it's normal to budget around 700 g/1½ lbs. crayfish per person, so most accept the imports! The main thing is that the crayfish has been cooked the Swedish way: in a brine, full of crown dill.

To host a traditional crayfish party, you first need a bunch of friends to celebrate with. If you can, host the crayfish party outside in the early autumn evening. Wear silly bibs and hats and decorate your garden with man-in-the-moon lanterns.

The crayfish – if purchased frozen, as most of it is these days – needs to be defrosted carefully in the fridge. Arrange all the crayfish on serving platters or trays and decorate with sprigs of crown dill and lemon.

As the main event really is the crayfish – and you traditionally celebrate with a shot of aquavit (the traditional Scandinavian spirit flavoured with spices and herbs) for each claw – it is advisable to serve bread alongside to fill up on. Most serve crusty bread, crisp bread, a huge lump of a good cheese, such as Västerbotten, and maybe a Västerbottenpaj (Västerbotten pie) or similar savoury pies.

To eat your crayfish, use your hands. Crack the head off – much like peeling a large prawn/shrimp. Connoisseurs happily make slurping noises as they suck the brine juices from the head of the crayfish. This is totally acceptable: eating crayfish is messy and loud! The main meat is the tail but you do find a bit of meat inside the claws, too. These can easily be got at with a nutcracker, or even your hands.

During the crayfish party, it is customary to sing 'Snapsvisor' (aquavit songs). After a few shots of the strong stuff, most people speak fluent Swedish and can usually sing along... or at least they think they can. Either way, by the end, you'll have made new friends and probably feel a bit more Swedish than when you arrived.

At our café, we host crayfish parties every year. We've helped introduce the custom to locals here in London since we opened, and it is one of our favourite times of the year, mainly because we get to bring out the trays of the little red beauties, wear our bibs and silly hats and play lots of ABBA on repeat.

Get together, eat loads of shellfish and sing happy songs. Bibs are very useful; the silly hats are optional.

MEATLOAF WITH HASSELBACK POTATOES

As far as I'm concerned, this is the ultimate home comfort dish and the meal I request when I go back to my parents' house in Denmark. It's a simple and easy-to-prepare meatloaf, but it's delicious with the sweet, creamy gravy and crisp potatoes. Traditionally, the meat used is half pork/beef – but my mother's recipe uses just beef; the result is a firmer meatloaf, but if you prefer a less firm loaf, use pork/beef.

80 g/¾ cup rolled/old-fashioned oats/

100 ml/7 tablespoons beef stock

500 g/1 lb 2 oz. minced/ground beef

1 small onion, grated

1 egg

1 teaspoon mustard

1 teaspoon tomato purée/paste

½ teaspoon ground allspice

salt and freshly ground black pepper

12–14 rashers/slices streaky/fatty bacon, thinly sliced

HASSELBACK POTATOES:

600 g/1 lb. 5 oz. roasting potatoes

50 g/3 tablespoons butter

50 g/1 scant cup dried breadcrumbs

SAUCE:

25 g/2 tablespoons butter

25 g/2 tablespoons plain/all-purpose flour

extra hot water or hot stock, as needed

salt and freshly ground black pepper

1–2 teaspoons redcurrant jelly or lingonberry jam/jelly

gravy browning (optional)

dash of cream

SERVES 4

Preheat the oven to 200°C (400°F) Gas 6.

Add the oats to the hot beef stock and leave to soak. In a food processor, add the beef and a good pinch of salt and start mixing. Add the onion to the meat, then the egg and spices. Add the soaked oats.

Turn out the meat, put it into an ovenproof dish and shape into a meatloaf. Cover the meatloaf with strips of bacon, ensuring that the whole loaf is covered. Pop into the preheated oven for 15 minutes on a high heat.

Meanwhile, prepare the potatoes. Using a sharp knife, cut slices two-thirds of the way through at close intervals (3–4 mm/⅛ in.) all the way across. Add to another ovenproof dish and drizzle with oil. Once the meatloaf has been in for 15 minutes, pop the potatoes in the oven, and turn the heat down to 175°C (350°F) Gas 4. Add 240 ml/1 cup water to the meatloaf dish.

After 20 minutes, melt the butter in a saucepan. Remove the potatoes from the oven. Brush each potato with the melted butter, season and scatter breadcrumbs on top. Return to the oven and cook for a further 20–25 minutes, after which the meatloaf and potatoes should be cooked. If the potatoes need a bit extra, remove the meatloaf from the oven and keep warm under foil.

To make the sauce, melt the butter in a saucepan, add the flour and whisk. Start adding the juices from the bottom of the meatloaf dish, adding more water when the mixture boils to make an even sauce (you may need to add extra water or stock). Taste the sauce and adjust the seasoning. Add the redcurrant jelly or lingonberry jam/jelly. Taste again, add the gravy browning (optional) and a dash of cream. The sauce should be a bit thicker than normal gravy, sweet but still balanced with salt and pepper.

Serve the meatloaf with the potatoes, sauce and seasonal vegetables.

REAL SWEDISH MEATBALLS

There are as many recipes for meatballs in Scandinavia as there are cooks. Recipes vary regionally, too, both in ingredients and sizing. Sadly, nowadays a lot of people buy meatballs instead of making them. The homemade version is so very wholesome and worth the effort. Serve with creamy mashed potato.

30 g/$\frac{1}{3}$ cup porridge/old-fashioned oats or breadcrumbs

150 ml/$\frac{2}{3}$ cup meat stock (chicken works well, too)

400 g/14 oz. minced/ground beef

250 g/9 oz. minced/ground pork (minimum 10% fat)

1 UK medium/US large egg

2$\frac{1}{2}$ tablespoons plain/all-purpose flour

pinch of salt

1 teaspoon ground allspice

$\frac{1}{2}$ teaspoon ground black pepper

$\frac{1}{2}$ teaspoon ground white pepper

a dash of Worcestershire sauce or soy sauce

1 small onion, grated

butter and oil, for frying

mashed potato, to serve

STIRRED LINGONBERRIES:

250 g/9 oz. frozen lingonberries (available in some speciality food stores and online)

100 g/$\frac{1}{2}$ cup caster/granulated sugar

CREAM GRAVY:

meat stock

1 tablespoon plain/all-purpose flour

a good glug of single/light cream

salt and ground black pepper

SERVES 6

If using oats, soak them in the meat or chicken stock for 5 minutes.

Mix the minced/ground meat with a good pinch of salt for a couple of minutes in a food processor to ensure it's blended thoroughly.

Add the eggs, flour, spices and Worcestershire or soy sauce to another bowl and mix with the soaked oats or breadcrumbs and grated onion, then add this to the meat mixture. You'll have a sticky, but moldable, mixture. Leave the mixture to rest for 20–25 minutes before using.

Heat up a frying pan/skillet with a small knob/pat or butter or oil and shape one small meatball. Fry it until done and then taste it. Adjust the seasoning according to taste and fry another meatball to test it until you get it just right.

Shape the individual meatballs in your hands – it helps if your hands are damp. Each meatball should be around 2.5 cm/1 in. in diameter, or larger if you haven't got time.

Melt a knob/pat of butter in a frying pan/skillet with a dash of oil and carefully add a few meatballs – make sure there is plenty of room for you to swivel the pan round and help turn them so they get a uniform round shape and do not stick. You'll most likely need to do this in several batches. Cooking time is usually around 5 minutes per batch. Keep in a warm oven until needed.

When your meatballs are done, keep the pan on a medium heat. Ensure you have enough fat in there, if not, add a knob/pat of butter to the pan. Add a tablespoon of flour and whisk, then add a splash of stock and whisk again as you bring to the boil. Keep adding stock until you have a good creamy gravy, then add a good dollop of single/light cream and season well with salt and pepper. The colour of the gravy should be very light brown.

To prepare the Stirred Lingonberries (rårörda lingon) simply add the caster/granulated sugar and stir. Leave for a while and then stir again, until the sugar dissolves and the berries have defrosted. Store leftover Stirred Lingonberries in the fridge.

Serve with mashed potatoes.

SAUTÉED REINDEER, CHANTERELLE MUSHROOMS AND GREEN BEANS

Usually sold in Scandinavian shops as 'Renskav', reindeer is cheap and extremely lean as a meat. Originating from Lapland, this super-tasty dish is an everyday meal in Sweden and other parts of Northern Scandinavia and is ready in minutes. Venison works as a substitute, but it will need to be thinly sliced.

100 g/3½ oz. fresh Chanterelle mushrooms or 10 g/⅓ oz. dried

1 small onion (approx. 70–80 g/2½–3 oz.)

20 g/1 tablespoon plus 1 teaspoon butter

400–500 g/14–18 oz. 'Renskav' shredded reindeer meat (usually available in 250 g/9 oz. packs in a speciality delicatessen) or venison

250 ml/1 cup stock, ideally game or mushroom

½ teaspoon dried thyme

15 g/1 tablespoon brown cheese or spreadable brown cheese (messmör)

100 ml/7 tablespoons double/heavy cream

salt and freshly ground black pepper

2–3 tablespoons Stirred Lingonberries, to taste (see page 92)

150 g/5½ oz. green beans, blanched and cut into bite-sized pieces.

chopped flat-leaf parsley, to garnish

SERVES 4

If using dried mushrooms, soak them for 10–15 minutes, then squeeze the excess water out. If using fresh chanterelles, dry-fry them for a few minutes in a hot frying pan/skillet to draw out the excess water (and set aside).

Finely slice the onion. In a saucepan, melt the butter and cook the onion until soft, taking care not to let it colour. Add the meat and fry it quickly until browned all over, then add the chanterelles and stir again.

Add the stock, thyme, brown cheese and cream and simmer for 5–8 minutes. Season with salt and pepper and the stirred lingonberries (taste the mixture – you may need more or fewer berries depending how sweet it is).

Lastly, add the green beans and parsley to garnish. If you have whole lingonberries, add a few on top, too – it looks very pretty!

This dish goes well with any type of potatoes (particularly a good creamy mash), rice or Seeded Rye Rolls (see page 135) along with pickles.

DANISH ROAST PORK (FLÆSKESTEG)

Go to a Danish house for Christmas and the chances are you will be served this wonderful dish alongside red cabbage (see Mamma Lena's Red Cabbage on page 98) and Caramelized Potatoes (see page 99).

1.2–1.4 kg/2¾–3 lbs. pork sirloin or loin, with the fat left on and scored almost to the flesh at 1-cm/½-in. sections crossways (so that every slice of roast gets a strip of crackling)

fine salt

sea salt

3 bay leaves

5 cloves (optional)

GRAVY:

3–5 tablespoons reserved fat

plain/all-purpose flour

potato or vegetable water

freshly ground black pepper

dollop of redcurrant jelly

salt and freshly ground black pepper

gravy browning (optional)

drop of Sherry (optional)

Marmite/yeast extract (optional)

single/light cream (optional)

meat thermometer (optional)

SERVES 6

Preheat the oven to 220°C (425°F) Gas 7.

Place the pork skin-side down in a baking pan and add enough hot water to cover the rind. Roast for 20 minutes in the preheated oven. This step ensures that the fat sections will separate and will help to produce superb crackling.

Discard the water and turn the meat over. Dry the rind with a paper towel. Sprinkle the fine salt liberally and add a generous spoonful of sea salt all over the rind. Add the bay leaves in 3 places (between the cuts in the rind). If using cloves, insert these into the rind, too.

Add 300 ml/1¼ cups of water to the bottom of the pan and return to the oven, reducing the temperature to 170°C (340°F) Gas 4. Roast for approximately 1 hour 20 minutes until the internal meat temperature reaches 68–70°C (154–158°F) (check with a meat thermometer), then remove the roast from the oven. Remove the cloves and bay leaves and discard. Remove the fat from the bottom of the pan and reserve for gravy, but baste the top of your crackling with a few spoonfuls first.

Turn a grill/broiler to high. Pop the roast back into the oven (middle to top), and watch it like a hawk while the crackling starts to splutter and crack. If one side starts to get too dark, add a piece of foil over that bit while you cook the rest. We never remove the crackling to cook it separately. We grill/broil, roast and turn it until the meat has an even crackling. The internal temperature of the pork should have risen to around 72–75°C (162–167°F) at this point and is ready. Leave it to stand for 15 minutes before carving. Be careful not to overcook the pork or it will be chewy and dry. If, on the other hand, the pork has not reached the right temperature, return it to the oven until it has.

The leftover juices make one of the tastiest gravies. Thicken some (3–5 tablespoons) of the reserved fat with plain/all-purpose flour and add potato or vegetable water to thin. Keep bringing to the boil and adding water until you have the desired consistency. Season and add the redcurrant jelly. Add gravy browning if needed. Additional seasoning may be required, depending on your meat. I usually add a small drop of Sherry, while my mother always adds a teaspoon of Marmite/yeast extract and a drop of single/light cream. The finished result should be a relatively thick, smooth gravy.

MAMMA LENA'S RED CABBAGE

Lena is my mother and she's the best cook in the world. Obviously. When I asked for her recipe for the lovely red cabbage she makes at home, her reply was – as it is with every recipe I ask her for – that she doesn't have a recipe, she just does whatever it is she usually does and it works out. So, I decided to watch her as she made it, making sure that I scribbled down exactly what she did!

1 head of red cabbage (approx. 1–1.25 kg/2¼–2¾ lbs.)

100 ml/7 tablespoons vinegar (I use apple cider vinegar)

200 ml/¾ cup plus 1 tablespoon water

2 teaspoons salt

2 tablespoons sugar

1 cinnamon stick

100 g/3½ oz. redcurrant or cranberry jelly

SERVES: 4-6 AS PART OF A MAIN MEAL

Remove the outer leaves and the core of the red cabbage, then finely shred the remaining leaves. Add them to a large saucepan along with the vinegar, water, salt, sugar and cinnamon. Leave to stew for a while with no lid and when the cooking has really begun (around 10 minutes), turn to a very low heat, pop the lid on and leave it alone for a while (although do keep checking if it is running dry of water – you will need to top it up frequently).

After about 1 hour, add a generous dollop of redcurrant or cranberry jelly. Taste and see if it needs more salt, sugar or vinegar – you need to keep tasting throughout the cooking time. The cabbage needs a balance of sweet, sour and salty.

Leave to cook for around 2–3 hours in total to allow the cabbage to really cook so it is very soft. Many recipes simply braise the cabbage so it is still crunchy – this is also delicious, but that is not the traditional way of cooking it. Season again at the end and it's ready (although it's always best the day after). This keeps very well in the fridge for over a week and can easily be reheated.

Serve with Danish Roast Pork (Flæskesteg) (see page 96). It's also great cold as a topping on open sandwiches with meatballs.

Tip: the red cabbage can be flavoured with different spices, such as cloves, bay leaves or orange peel.

CARAMELIZED BABY POTATOES

There is no way to convince anyone that this is a healthy side dish, which is probably why we only really eat it at Christmas and on special occasions. It's utterly delicious with Flæskesteg (Danish Roast Pork) or roast duck and worth every bite.

1 kg/2¼ lbs. small potatoes

80 g/¼ cup plus 2 tablespoons caster/granulated sugar

25 g/2 tablespoons butter

SERVES: 6 AS PART OF A MAIN MEAL (MORE, IF ALSO SERVING WITH BOILED POTATOES, WHICH I OFTEN DO TO MAKE THE MEAL LESS SUGAR-HEAVY)

The day before: boil the potatoes until just done – take great care not to overcook them, though or the final dish will not work. Once the potatoes are cooked, peel off the skin carefully (this is a fiddly job – alternatively, peel the potatoes before boiling). Leave the potatoes in the fridge overnight.

The next day, mix the sugar with 50 ml/3 tablespoons water.

Heat up a frying pan/skillet, and once it's very hot, add the sugar mixture. Leave to bubble for 3–5 minutes or until you can tell the water has evaporated (the mixture will start to go a bit thicker). Add the butter and leave to melt.

After 3–4 minutes, the mixture will start to caramelize and turn brown. At this point, add the potatoes and swirl around. Keep the heat high so the caramel remains liquid as you coat the potatoes.

Slowly reduce the heat, bit by bit; the caramel will start to form a thin sticky layer around the potatoes. The whole process will take around 10 minutes from this stage – keep adjusting the heat to ensure the caramel is fluid enough to stick to the potatoes as you turn them in the frying pan/skillet (the idea is to coat the potatoes with a thin layer of caramel, not end up with a caramel gravy).

Note: Traditionally, most cooks will start by browning the sugar and add a splash of water to the hot pan. I find this rather risky as it splutters a great deal. Recent tests in the Danish cooking world also agree that adding the sugar and water together first is a safe method of making this dish and gives the same result.

SAVOY CABBAGE PARCELS (KÅLDOLMAR)

When Swedish King Charles XII returned to Sweden in 1715 after spending five years in the Ottoman Empire, his aides are said to have brought back this dish, what has now become a Swedish classic. Vine leaves were very expensive in Sweden, and the first printed Kåldolmar recipe states that it is acceptable to substitute with boiled cabbage leaves. Over the years, the dish has been further Scandi-fied with the use of pork or beef – and it is served with a good dollop of Stirred Lingonberries (see page 92) and a rich potato mash.

1 large head of Savoy cabbage (or white cabbage) – you may need two heads, if small

vegetable oil, for frying

MEAT MIXTURE:

250 g/9 oz. minced/ground pork

250 g/9 oz. minced/ground beef

1 teaspoon coarse salt

50 g/1 scant cup dried breadcrumbs

150 ml/$\frac{1}{2}$ cup plus 2 tablespoons milk

1 medium potato, cooked

1 small onion, finely chopped

1 egg

$\frac{1}{2}$ teaspoon ground allspice

$\frac{1}{2}$ teaspoon fresh nutmeg

2 tablespoons soy sauce

salt and freshly ground black pepper

SAUCE:

knob/pat of butter

50 g/1$\frac{3}{4}$oz. cubed bacon

100 g/3$\frac{1}{2}$ oz. celeriac

1 carrot

500 ml/2 cups meat stock (chicken works well)

string or cocktail sticks/toothpicks

MAKES 20

To make the meat mixture, add the pork, beef and salt to a stand mixer and mix well. Soak the breadcrumbs in the milk for a few minutes. Mash the cooked potato with a fork and add to the milk and mix. Add to the meat along with the other ingredients and mix well. Transfer to a bowl and cover. Allow to rest in the fridge for at least 30 minutes before using.

Cut the main bit of stalk out of the base of the cabbage and try to separate the leaves slightly without breaking them.

Steam or boil the cabbage until the leaves are soft – this can take anything from 5–10 minutes. Carefully separate the leaves out – you need roughly 20 good-sized unbroken leaves.

Place approximately 60–65 g/2 oz. meat in each leaf and wrap it up like a parcel. Secure with string or a cocktail stick/toothpick. You may need to cut away the bottom bit of hard stalk before wrapping the meat up.

Preheat then oven to 180°C (350°F) Gas 4.

Heat the butter in a frying pan/skillet and cook the bacon. Chop the celeriac and carrot into small cubes and cook for a few minutes until soft. Remove from pan/skillet and set aside.

Heat a few tablespoons of oil in the pan/skillet and fry the cabbage parcels on each side for a minute. Arrange the parcels in an ovenproof dish and scatter over the vegetables and three-quarters of the meat stock. Brush the parcels with a bit of melted butter.

Cook in the preheated oven for 30–40 minutes or until cooked through. Continue to baste the parcels as you cook to prevent them going dry. Add more stock if needed.

Serve with mashed potatoes and Stirred Lingonberries (see page 92). Use the stock as a sauce (season to taste before serving).

Our countries are a wonderful mix of beautiful old and stylish new.

DESSERTS

A hearty meal with friends and family calls for a good dessert to support it. In the summer, our desserts are made of berries and sunlight (pretty much) – there is little need to mess with what Mother Nature provides in the lighter months. During the colder, darker months, we're all about crumbles and tarts and compotes, using the late summer fruits and preserving them until spring comes around again.

TRADITIONAL DANISH APPLE TRIFLE

Growing up in Denmark, our garden was full of apple trees and my mother would make this dessert a lot, as we always had cases and cases of apples to get through in the autumn months. A spoonful of this dessert sends me straight back to her warm kitchen...

1 kg/2 lbs. 3 oz. (approx. 8–10) tart apples, such as Bramley or Granny Smith, peeled and cored

140 g/¾ cup caster/granulated sugar

200 ml/¾ cup plus 1 tablespoon water

seeds from 1 vanilla pod/bean

100 g/1 stick minus 1 tablespoon butter

120 g/2 cups dried breadcrumbs

300 ml/1¼ cups whipping cream

SERVES 4

Cut the apples into bite-sized pieces. Add them to a saucepan along with 4 tablespoons sugar, the water and vanilla and cook over a gentle heat until completely soft – around 20 minutes. Add more water if needed during cooking. Leave to cool completely.

In a frying pan/skillet, melt the butter, then add the remaining sugar and stir. Add the breadcrumbs and keep stirring until the mixture is toasted through. Be careful, though, because the breadcrumbs burn easily.

When crispy, remove from the heat and spread on a plate. As the breadcrumbs cool, use your fingers to ensure that they don't stick in clumps.

Whip the cream until stiff peaks form.

Layer your trifle, beginning with a layer of apple, then the breadcrumbs followed by a layer of cream. Add a larger layer of apple and finish with the breadcrumbs (save a few to decorate). Top with the remaining whipped cream and decorate with the remaining breadcrumbs.

Opinion is divided about when to serve this. Some people prefer to serve it straight away while the breadcrumbs are still crunchy. However, in Mamma Lena's kitchen, we wait a few hours until the trifle has settled.

A great no-bake dessert that everybody loves. Make either in individual serving pots or in a big glass trifle bowl.

WHIPPED LINGONBERRIES (VISPIPUURO)

This is a dessert, but it can be eaten at any time of the day. Deliciously sweet and fruity, it really brings out the best in the lingonberries. You can use fresh or frozen berries for this – and if you don't have lingonberries, try it with other berries. The secret to a good Vispipuuro is all in the whipping of the semolina once it has cooled down. This will turn the dessert from quite heavy into a fluffy consistency.

200 g/7 oz. lingonberries

500 ml/2 cups water

80 g/5 tablespoons caster/granulated sugar

65 g/4 tablespoons semolina

drop of vanilla extract or vanilla sugar

milk or single/light cream, to serve

fresh raspberries, to serve

SERVES 4

Place the lingonberries in a saucepan with the water and sugar and bring to the boil.

Simmer for about 10-15 minutes until the berries are cooked through, then pour through a sieve/strainer, preserving the juice. Press most of the berries into the juice, but discard the skins. Leave some whole for decoration.

Pour the liquid back into the pan and add the semolina and vanilla extract or sugar. Bring back to the boil and simmer for 5-6 minutes until cooked through and thickened.

Take the semolina mixture off the boil and leave to cool down. Once warm, use an electric whisk on full speed to whip it for about 10 minutes. After a few minutes, it will change colour from dark purple to pink, and the texture becomes light.

Serve cold in a bowl with milk (or single/light cream) and with the reserved lingonberries and fresh raspberries on top.

This dish also works well for a breakfast treat. You can always make it healthier by reducing the amount of sugar and increasing the quantity of berries.

Enjoy this as a dessert – or even as a breakfast. Or just a snack. It works at any time!

GLÖGG PEAR AND MAZARIN TART

Mazarin is a baked cake filling widely used in Scandinavian baking and pastries. It is not unlike frangipane, but we make it using marzipan/almond paste and flour.

GLÖGG PEARS:

3–4 firm and not too ripe pears, peeled and cored

500 ml/2 cups Glögg (see page 141)

DOUGH:

150 g 1¼ sticks cold butter

220 g /1²⁄₃ cups plain/all-purpose flour

50 g/generous ⅓ cup icing/confectioners' sugar, sifted

1 egg

MAZARIN FILLING:

100 g/1 stick minus 1 tablespoon butter, cubed

100 g/½ cup sugar

1 teaspoon vanilla sugar

150 g/5½ oz. marzipan/almond paste (ideally 50% pure), cut into small pieces; to make homemade marzipan/almond paste (see note, below right)

2 eggs

60 g/½ cup plain/all-purpose flour

1½ teaspoons cocoa powder

toasted almond flakes/slivers, to decorate

28-cm/11-in. loose-based tart pan

SERVES 8

First make the dough: cut the butter into cubes and add to a food processor with flour, icing/confectioners' sugar and egg. Pulse until it just comes together. When the dough has a good, even consistency, shape it into a ball with your hands, taking care not to overwork it. Wrap in clingfilm/plastic wrap and let it rest in the fridge for 30 minutes before using.

To prepare the pears, pour the Glögg (mulled wine) into a saucepan. Place the pears in the wine. Pop a lid on the saucepan, bring to the boil and then turn off, leaving the pears to stand in the wine until completely cold (overnight is fine).

To make the mazarin filling, cream the butter, sugar and vanilla sugar together. Add the marzipan (in pieces) and keep whisking until incorporated and creamy. Add the eggs one at the time, beating well. Fold the flour and cocoa powder into the mixture with a spatula, making sure it is thoroughly combined.

Dust the kitchen table with flour and roll out the tart dough to the shape of your tart pan, rolling it slightly larger so that it covers all sides. When the pan is lined, place it in the fridge or freezer for 15 minutes to chill.

Preheat the oven to 180°C (350°F) Gas 4.

Prick the base of the pastry tart lightly with a fork, place a piece of baking parchment inside and add a layer of baking beans. Bake blind in the preheated oven for 10 minutes.

Remove the pears from the wine. Cut each pear into 4 lengthways slices, ensuring you do not cut all the way to the top so you can 'fan' out the slices a little when placing them on the filling. Spread the filling evenly over the tart base. Arrange the pears in a pattern all the way round on top of the filling.

Bake the tart in the middle of the oven for 20–25 minutes. Before serving, sprinkle with the almond flakes/slivers.

Note: To make marzipan/almond paste, combine 200 g/7 oz. ground almonds, 100 g/½ cup caster/granulated sugar, 100 g/²⁄₃ cup icing/confectioners' sugar, 1 (pasteurized) egg white and 1 tablespoon almond essence in a food processor and blitz. Knead together until smooth and allow to settle in the fridge before using.

CREAMED RICE PUDDING WITH WARM CHERRY SAUCE

One of the most popular and traditional Christmas desserts, this is a creamy cold pudding, served at the Christmas meal on 24th December. Include a single whole almond in the rice – the lucky person who finds it should receive a gift, usually a box of fancy chocolates. It's best to make the rice pudding the day before you assemble the dish but this isn't essential.

RICE PUDDING:

300 ml/2¼ cups water

200 g/1 cup pudding rice (short-grained white rice)

1 litre/4 cups whole milk

1 vanilla pod/bean

salt

TO ASSEMBLE:

100 g/3½ oz. blanched almonds

50 g/3 tablespoons icing/confectioners' sugar

300 ml/1¾ cups whipping cream

CHERRY SAUCE:

2 x 300–350 g/10½–12½ oz.) cans morello or black cherries in syrup (retain 250 ml/1 cup cherry syrup from the can)

2 heaped tablespoons cornflour/cornstarch

1 teaspoon orange juice

2–3 tablespoons rum

SERVES 8

Add the water and rice to a thick-bottomed saucepan. Bring to the boil and cook for about 2 minutes, stirring continuously. Cut the vanilla pod/bean, scrape out the seeds and add to the rice (throw in the pod/bean too, for flavour).

Turn the heat down to low and add the milk. Cook for about 10 minutes, stirring frequently to avoid it burning and sticking to the pan. Turn the heat down to a very low heat, cover and simmer for 25 minutes, stirring occasionally (or until the rice is cooked). Keep an eye on it, because it can burn easily.

Once the rice is cooked, remove the rice pudding from the heat and add salt, to taste. Leave to chill, ideally overnight.

To assemble the dish, roughly chop the almonds, apart from one, which should be kept whole. Set aside.

Remove the vanilla pod/bean, add the sugar and chopped almonds and stir. Add a dash of water if the pudding has set too firmly.

In a separate bowl, lightly whip the cream to peaks, then fold into the rice pudding. Add the whole almond and chill until serving.

For the cherry sauce, combine a small amount of the syrup with the cornflour/cornstarch to make a roux, and set aside. In a saucepan, bring the cherries and the rest of the juice to the boil, then add the roux, stirring constantly. Allow to boil for a minute for the cornflour/cornstarch taste to disappear. Turn the heat to low until you're ready to serve the sauce so it doesn't continue to boil. Taste to see if more sugar is required. Season to taste with orange juice and rum to balance the flavours.

MINI PRINCESS CAKES

Sometimes, we like to make the large traditional Swedish Princess Cake into little individual desserts, which increases the wow-factor of this amazing cake.

2 x cake layers (see page 116) or ready-bought sponge layers

200 ml/1 cup whipping cream

½ x quantity of Crème Pâtissière (see below)

4 tablespoons raspberry jam/preserve

1 tablespoon icing/confectioners' sugar, plus extra to dust

200 g/7 oz. marzipan/almond paste (see page 110), coloured green with colouring paste

200 g/2 cups fresh raspberries

MAKES 6

Using a cookie cutter with a diameter of 4–5 cm/1½–2 in., cut out 18 round circles from the cake layers.

Whip the cream until stiff peaks form and mix with the Crème Pâtissière. Chill in the fridge until required.

Spread a thin layer of jam/preserve on 12 of the cake circles. On 6 of the jam/preserve-covered bases, pipe out the Crème Pâtissière mixture (around 1 cm/½ in. high), then place the remaining 6 jam/preserve-covered cakes on top. Repeat with the Crème Pâtissière layer and then add the final cake layer.

Make a template from baking parchment measuring roughly 15 x 6 cm/6 x 2½ in. Dust the worktop with icing/confectioners´ sugar and then roll out your marzipan/almond paste in long strips and cut 6 pieces, using the template. The marzipan/almond paste should be 1 cm/½ in. taller than the cake layers and quite thinly rolled. Wrap the marzipan/almond paste around each cake, pipe a small amount of the Crème Pâtissière on top of each and then fill the top with raspberries. Dust with icing/confectioners´ sugar before serving.

CRÈME PÂTISSIÈRE

Many recipes in Scandinavian baking use crème pâtissière – from layer cakes to baked goods and Danish pastries. This is a simple, quick and delicious version.

500 ml/2 cups whole milk

½ vanilla pod/bean

2 eggs

100 g /½ cup caster/granulated sugar

30 g/¼ cup cornflour/cornstarch

½ teaspoon salt

25 g/2 tablespoons butter

Heat the milk in a saucepan together with the scraped out vanilla seeds. Add the whole pod/bean to the pan, too, for extra flavour.

In a bowl, whisk together the eggs, sugar, cornflour/cornstarch and salt. When the milk reaches boiling point, remove the vanilla pod/bean and discard, and pour in a quarter of the hot milk into the egg mixture, whisking as you do so. Once whisked through, pour the egg mixture back into the remaining hot milk, return to the heat and bring to the boil, whisking continuously. Let it bubble for just under a minute. Make sure you whisk as it thickens.

Remove from the heat and add the butter, whisking in well. Pour into a cold bowl, then cover the top with a sheet of baking parchment to prevent a hard edge from forming as it cools down. Place in the fridge to cool completely.

MIDSUMMER

Scandinavia is a dark and cold place during the winter months (with some places never even seeing daylight for several months), so when the days get lighter, we like to be outside as much as possible. Ever seen cows dance when put out to graze after a long winter cooped up inside the barn? That's a bit like us at Midsummer. In essence, it is all about celebrating the summer and the fertility of the season and all that Mother Nature gives us: light, food and a surge in hormones. It is perhaps not a coincidence that every year in Sweden, the birth rate surges around nine months after Midsummer.

Danes, Swedes and Norwegians don't all celebrate Midsummer in the same way. Danes and Norwegians celebrate St. Hans (the feast of St. John) on the 23rd June each year by gathering around huge bonfires on the beach. In Denmark, they put straw witches on the bonfire – an old tradition of 'sending the witch to the German mountains'. Then they sing songs about how much they love Denmark and bake stick-bread on the bonfire. There may or may not be some skinny dipping, too. In Sweden, Midsummer is always marked on the nearest Friday. The importance of Midsummer completely overshadows Swedish National Day just a few weeks earlier: Midsummer is THE celebration of the summer and the one that everybody takes part in. At our café, it is one of the biggest celebrations of the year.

People always gather outside for Midsummer. Girls put on floaty dresses and wear flower garlands in their hair, and everybody looks wonderfully summery and very blonde, like an advert for fabric softener. Matjes herring is eaten and aquavit is drunk. Maypoles are decorated with flowers and there is dancing around the pole. Hands are held, songs are sung – the most famous of which is 'Små grodorna' (Little Frogs), a song about being a little tadpole with no ears and legs. People jump up and down and generally fall about, laughing.

We Scandinavians are a funny lot: our countries are geographically so close that our traditions and beliefs overlap, but we're so far apart when it comes to what makes each corner of Scandinavia unique. Nevertheless, what binds us all together, without fail, is the excellent produce and food found across the region. Midsummer is the perfect opportunity to create a beautiful Scandinavian Smörgåsbord of summery delicacies from your chosen region, from dill-cured salmon to delicately pickled herring and an abundance of shellfish to the season's new potatoes, tossed in fresh dill. For some of us ex-pat Scandinavians, there is something magical about the first crop of new potatoes from the soil where you grew up: they just taste different. They taste of home, of all the summers you ran across fields chasing your own tail and trying desperately to escape exactly what you're now trying to bring back as an adult. Add to that some nice Scandinavian bread, a few shots of aquavit and you're ready to celebrate. Welcome, summer – and good riddance to you, long dark winter.

It's the day when the sun doesn't set and we sit outside, enjoying nature and all that she gives us.

STRAWBERRY SUMMER LAYER CAKE

In Sweden, this cake is called 'Jordgubbstårta' and it's got all the flavours of a Nordic summer. Don't be put off by the components: the process is surprisingly easy!

1 x quantity Crème Pâtissière (see page 113), cooled in the fridge

CAKE LAYERS:

3 eggs

90 g/scant ½ cup caster/granulated sugar

90 g/⅔ cup plain/all-purpose flour

1 teaspoon vanilla sugar

20 g/4 teaspoons melted butter

WHIPPED CREAM:

600 ml/2¾ cups whipping cream

2 tablespoons icing/confectioners' sugar, plus extra to dust

1 teaspoon vanilla sugar

ASSEMBLING THE CAKE:

75 g/¼ cup raspberry jam/preserve

600 g/6 cups strawberries, washed, trimmed and sliced

3 baking sheets greased and lined with baking parchment

piping bag fitted with a star nozzle/tip

SERVES 6-8

Preheat the oven to 200°C (400°F) Gas 6.

Trace 3 identical circles approximately 20 cm/8 in. in diameter (use a plate as a guide) onto the baking parchment-lined baking sheets. If you wish, you can bake the cake layers in two batches as they only need to be in the oven for a short while.

To make the cake layers, whisk the eggs and sugar until white and fluffy. The key here is to whisk for a long time to incorporate as much air as possible. Sift the flour and vanilla sugar into the egg mixture and fold, very carefully, until completely incorporated. Fold thoroughly but very gently in order to preserve as much air as possible. Lastly, add the melted butter and stir carefully.

Using a spatula, carefully divide the batter between the 3 circles and ensure the batter neatly fills the circles all the way around. Bake in the preheated oven until just golden brown and done – this will depend on your oven, but 5–6 minutes is usually fine. Remove from the oven and leave to cool completely on a cooling rack. When cool, very carefully remove the baking parchment – if it sticks, wet the back of the paper a little bit and it should come off easily.

Whisk the whipped cream ingredients until stiff peaks form. Fold one-third of the whipped cream together with the Crème Pâtissière until completely incorporated (the remaining whipped cream is used to decorate the final cake).

To assemble the cake, place the first layer cake on the plate you wish to serve on. Spread a layer of raspberry jam/preserve, followed by a generous layer of the Crème Pâtissière mixture. Add a good handful of sliced strawberries, evenly spread out. Add another cake layer, then the raspberry jam/preserve, Crème Pâtissière and strawberries again, and place the final cake layer on top. Trim any excess cream away from the edges of the cake with a spatula. Using a palette knife, spread a thin layer of the whipped cream on the top of the cake. Add the rest of the cream to a piping bag and pipe carefully around the edge of the cake in an up-and-down motion until the sides are covered. If you do not have a piping bag, you can use the palette knife for this and just smooth the edges.

Finish by adding the remaining strawberries on the top of the cake. It doesn't have to look too arranged – just scatter them so the cake is evenly covered. Dust with icing/confectioners' sugar. Serve with lots of sunshine!

DANISH SWEET SUMMER SOUP WITH 'KAMMERJUNKER' BISCUITS

This refreshing cold dessert signifies the height of summer to Danes. Kammerjunker biscuits are crisp, sweet biscuits/cookies, lightly crushed or added whole to the soup. They need to be really crispy to carry the lightness of the soup.

BISCUITS/COOKIES:

150 g/1 cup plus 1 tablespoon plain/all-purpose flour

1 teaspoon baking powder

50 g/¼ cup caster/granulated sugar

50 g/3 tablespoons cold butter

1 egg

1 teaspoon vanilla extract

½ teaspoon ground cardamom (optional)

zest from ½ lemon

2 teaspoons single/light cream

SOUP:

2 egg yolks (pasteurized, ideally – this soup contains raw egg yolk)

60 g/⅓ cup caster/granulated sugar

seeds from 1 vanilla pod/bean

zest from ½ lemon

150 ml/⅔ cup Greek or natural yogurt

1 litre/4 cups buttermilk

freshly squeezed juice from ¼ lemon

TO SERVE:
strawberries, quartered

baking sheet lined with parchment

SERVES 4

To make the biscuits/cookies, combine the flour with the baking powder. Add the cold butter, cubed, and mix in until you have grainy result. Add the sugar, then the other ingredients and mix again until you have an even dough. Wrap in clingfilm/plastic wrap and chill in the fridge for 20 minutes.

Preheat the oven to 200°C (400°F) Gas 6.

Roll the dough out and cut 35–40 small pieces, roll them into balls and place them on the lined baking sheet.

Bake for 7–10 minutes in the preheated oven, depending on your oven. Remove and cut each biscuit/cookie across the middle so you end up with two flat halves.

Turn down the oven to 170°C (350°F) Gas 4.

Place the biscuits/cookies on the lined baking sheet and return to to the warm oven. Bake for a further 8–10 minutes or until golden and crisp. Allow to cool on a wire rack.

To make the soup, whisk the egg yolk and sugar until white in a food processor on a high setting. Add the vanilla and lemon zest, then the yogurt and buttermilk whilst continuously whisking. Add lemon juice to taste – the soup should be sweet but have a good lemon flavour coming through.

Serve the cold soup in bowls, topped with strawberries and pieces of the biscuits/cookies.

Tip: This soup should be eaten on day of making it as it contains raw egg. However, if there are any leftovers, I use the soup mixed in with a fresh fruit smoothie the morning after: it's delicious.

APPLE AND CLOUDBERRY CRUMBLE

The humble cloudberry is probably the most sought-after berry in the Nordic countries. Very difficult to cultivate, the berries mostly grow in the wild far north and have a short season lasting only a few weeks. Cloudberries grow on stalks and look a bit like raspberries, although orange in colour. The berries are rich in vitamin C and antioxidants – and if you eat them fresh, you will find them sharp in flavour. Most cloudberries are made into jams that are used in desserts.

6 Granny Smith apples (or equivalent tart apples)

2 tablespoons freshly squeezed lemon juice

seeds from 1/2 vanilla pod/bean

200 g/2/3 cup cloudberry jam/preserve

vanilla ice cream or fresh vanilla custard, to serve

CRUMBLE TOPPING:

100 g/3/4 cup plain/all-purpose flour

80 g/3/4 cup ground almonds

40 g/1/4 cup chopped hazelnuts or almonds

100 g/7 tablespoons butter

100 g/1/2 cup golden caster/granulated sugar

a pinch of sea salt

flaked/slivered almonds (optional)

SERVES 4–6

Preheat the oven to 180°C (350°F) Gas 4.

Peel and core the apples and cut into bite-sized pieces. Place in a saucepan with a dash of water. Heat and stir for a few minutes, then add the lemon juice and vanilla. Turn off the heat and fold in the cloudberry jam/preserve (if you are lucky and you can get hold of fresh cloudberries, use half cloudberries and half cloudberry jam/preserve, but reduce the amount of lemon juice a bit as fresh cloudberries are very tart).

To make the crumble topping, blitz all the ingredients apart from the flaked/slivered almonds in a food processor, until you have a crumbly mixture.

Add the apples to an ovenproof dish and top evenly with the crumble mixture. Add flaked/slivered almonds, if using, to the top of the crumble for extra crunch.

Bake in the preheated oven 180°C (350°F) Gas 4 for about 25–30 minutes or until cooked.

Serve with a good vanilla ice cream or vanilla custard.

There are few
things more
satisfying
than a cycle
ride through
a Danish forest
in the spring.

BAKES

The smell of cinnamon and cardamom take me back to my family kitchen. Learning to bake as a child means I always find comfort in baking, from the kneading of bread to the dusting of sugar on cakes. Whenever I have any problems that need solving, I start by making a big batch of dough that needs kneading. It's quite amazing what can be solved through baking.

SEED CRISPBREAD

For those of us who stick to a no-gluten way of eating, having a recipe for a crispbread that isn't hard to make is really useful. This easy crispbread is full of seed goodness, too. My mother-in-law Eva kindly shared her recipe for this crispbread and we have since adapted it with extra seeds and buckwheat flour. If you don't worry about the gluten, you can use plain/all-purpose flour instead of the naturally gluten-free buckwheat flour (in this case, you can also omit the xanthan gum).

50 g/¼ cup sesame seeds

70 g/½ cup sunflower seeds

70 g/½ cup pumpkin seeds

50 g/½ cup flaxseeds/linseeds

20 g/1 tablespoon plus 1 teaspoon chia seeds

50 g/⅓ cup buckwheat flour

pinch of xanthan gum

50 ml/3½ tablespoons rapeseed/canola oil

150 ml/⅔ cup boiling water

pinch of sea salt, plus extra for sprinkling

2 large baking sheets, greased and lined with baking parchment

MAKES 2 LARGE SHEETS (ROUGHLY 20 SMALLER PIECES)

Preheat the oven to 150°C (300°F) Gas 2.

Combine all the ingredients in a bowl and stir. You will have a jelly-like consistency mixture, not a dough.

Place half the mixture on one sheet of baking parchment. Place another sheet of baking parchment on top and roll out as evenly and thinly as possible. Carefully remove the parchment. The mixture will remain sticky.

Repeat on the second baking sheet. Sprinkle a little extra salt to the top of each and place in the oven.

Bake for 50–60 minutes until crispy and completely baked through.

Remove from oven and allow to cool slightly before breaking into large pieces. Store in an airtight container.

DANISH RYE BREAD

Every baking household in Denmark has a recipe for rye bread, usually with a long history to it. This one is from my little sister Ulla, who got it from her best friend who got it from her mother who got it from her aunt... and so the tradition carries on... If you don't have a sourdough starter, follow the instructions to make one from scratch.

DAY 1 INGREDIENTS:

100 ml/7 tablespoons water

100 g/1 scant cup rye flour

DAY 6 INGREDIENTS:

4 tablespoons sourdough starter

150 ml/^{2}/$_3$ cup water

150 g/1 cup plus 2 tablespoons rye flour

DAY 7 INGREDIENTS:

300 ml/1^1/$_4$ cups sourdough starter

1 litre/4 cups lukewarm water

2 tablespoons salt

750 g/5^1/$_3$ cups dark rye flour

250 g/1^3/$_4$ cups white strong/bread flour

DAY 8 INGREDIENTS:

500 g/2^1/$_2$ cups chopped rye kernels/rye grain

100 g/^{3}/$_4$ cup sunflower seeds

100 g/^{3}/$_4$ cup flaxseeds/linseeds

1 tablespoon dark syrup or dark corn syrup

2 tablespoons barley malt syrup

1 teaspoon barley malt powder

300 ml/1^1/$_4$ cups lukewarm water or malt beer

1.8-kg/4-lb. traditional rye bread pan

MAKES 1

Days 1–6 (making a starter): Mix the Day 1 ingredients together and leave in tub on kitchen counter, lightly covered. Stir daily. In 4–5 days, it will start to bubble. On Day 6, add the ingredients to the starter and stir with a non-metal spoon. Leave for another 12–18 hours and the starter should be ready to use (you should see some serious bubbling action – if not, wait a bit longer).

Day 7: Take 300 ml/1^1/$_4$ cups of the starter and mix it with the other Day 7 ingredients. Leave in a bowl on your kitchen counter, covered with clingfilm/plastic wrap, for 24 hours.

Day 8: Remove 300 ml/1^1/$_4$ cups of the dough and place in a tub in fridge for next time you bake (this is your starter going forward). Mix the rest of the dough with the Day 8 ingredients in a stand mixer on low speed for around 10 minutes. The dough will be sticky and gloopy, like a thick oatmeal porridge.

Grease and line the rye bread pan. Fill the pan no more than three-quarters full, cover with clingfilm/plastic wrap and leave for another 8 hours on the kitchen table.

Preheat the oven to its hottest setting, around 250°C (475°F) Gas 9.

With a fork, prick the top of the rye bread all over. Brush with water and pop into the oven, immediately turning it down to 180°C (350°F) Gas 4. Bake for 1–1^1/$_2$ hours or until the internal temperature reaches 98°C (208°F) – the baking time will vary depending on your pan and oven.

Remove the loaf from the pan and cover with a damp dish towel to ensure that a very hard crust does not form as it cools.

Store in a plastic bag to keep the loaf soft. Leave 24 hours before eating as the bread needs to settle.

Note: Feed your starter in the fridge: once or twice a week, add a few spoonfuls of rye flour and an equal quantity of water to keep it alive. When you want to bake more, start from Day 7 again.

EASY DANISH RYE BREAD

If you have a sourdough starter, you should make real Danish rye bread using that, because the traditional way is the best. However, if – like me – you don't have any sourdough alive in your fridge, then there are ways to get around it without having to wait for days before you can bake a new loaf. Use a soured dairy product such as buttermilk to get the right taste, and the rye kernels/grain must be chopped or cut – if they are whole, it won't work.

300 ml/1¼ cups buttermilk

150 ml/⅔ cup water

25 g/1 oz. fresh yeast
or 13 g/2½ teaspoons dried/
active dry yeast

50 g/¼ cup kibbled/
cracked rye kernels/rye
grain, chopped (these can be
replaced by sunflower seeds if
you don't have rye kernels)

500 g/3½ cups dark rye flour

100 g/¾ cup white strong/
bread flour

1 tablespoon salt

1 teaspoon barley malt
powder

1 tablespoon barley malt syrup
or dark syrup

50 g/½ cup flaxseeds/
linseeds

50 g/1¼ cups sunflower seeds

*1.8-kg/4-lb. traditional rye
bread pan or 2 x 900-g/
2-lb. loaf pans*

**MAKES 1 LOAF OR
2 SMALLER ONES**

If using fresh yeast, heat the buttermilk and water to finger-warm temperature (36–37°C/97–98°F). Add the yeast and warmed buttermilk and water to a food mixer with the dough hook attached and mix until the yeast has dissolved.

If using dried/active dry yeast, heat the water to finger-warm temperature (36–37°C/97–98°F) and pour into a bowl. Sprinkle on the yeast and whisk together. Cover with clingfilm/plastic wrap and leave in a warm place for about 15 minutes to activate and become frothy and bubbly. Gently warm the buttermilk to finger-warm temperature. Pour the yeast and buttermilk into the food mixer with the dough hook attached.

In a saucepan, boil the rye kernels/rye berries for 3–4 minutes, then drain and set aside to cool.

Add the flours, salt, barley malt powder, barley malt syrup (or dark syrup), seeds and rye kernels. Knead for 5 minutes until the dough is thoroughly mixed. If the dough is too dry, add a little water. Too wet, a little extra flour. This will depend on the flour you use. Cover the bowl with clingfilm/plastic wrap and leave the dough to rise for 40 minutes.

Knead the dough again, then shape into a loaf (or two) and add to the pan(s). If using non-stick pan(s), don't forget to oil them. Cover and leave to rise for another 20–25 minutes.

Preheat the oven to 180°C (350°F) Gas 4.

Brush the top of each loaf with water and use a fork to prick holes across the surface. This prevents the crust from rising up unevenly.

Place in the preheated oven and bake for 1 hour 15 minutes (for a large loaf) and 40–45 minutes (for smaller loaves). The general rule of thumb is that the bread is baked when the internal temperature is 98°C (208°F). Remove from the oven and turn out onto a wire rack, then cover the loaf or loaves with a slightly damp dish towel to prevent a hard crust from forming. Leave to cool completely before slicing.

MORMOR'S CARAWAY LOAF

Mormor means 'grandmother' in Scandinavia. My mormor's house always had a faint scent of caraway – my morfar (grandfather) was a famous cheesemaker and his speciality was a young soft cheese, smoked over nettles and hay and topped with caraway seeds. This easy caraway loaf reminds me of her house and all the lovely cheeses we used to eat there.

25 g/1 oz. fresh yeast or 13 g/ 2½ teaspoons active dry yeast

100 ml/7 tablespoons finger-warm water (36–37°C/97–98°F)

250 ml/1 cup buttermilk, at room temperature

1 tablespoon sugar

1 teaspoon salt

2 teaspoons caraway seeds, plus extra for topping

1 teaspoon fennel seeds, lightly crushed

300 g/2 cups wholegrain spelt flour

150–200 g/1–1½ cups white strong/bread flour

beaten egg, for brushing

450-g/1-lb. bread pan, greased and lined with baking parchment

MAKES 1 LOAF

If using fresh yeast, add it to the warm water and stir until the yeast has dissolved.

If using active dry yeast, pour the finger-warm water into a bowl, sprinkle on the yeast and whisk together. Cover with clingfilm/plastic wrap and leave in a warm place for about 15 minutes to activate and become frothy and bubbly.

Pour the yeast mixture into a large bowl. Add the buttermilk and sugar, then the salt and stir well. Add the caraway seeds and fennel seeds. Add the mixture to a food mixer with a dough hook attached, and start adding the spelt flour bit by bit while mixing on a low setting. Keep adding until all the spelt flour has been kneaded in, then start adding the strong/bread flour. You may or may not need all of it (or you may need a bit more) – this depends on the strength of your flour. Knead on low speed for around 7–8 minutes. Your dough should be elastic and firm, but not dry.

Place the dough in a bowl, cover with clingfilm/plastic wrap and leave to rise for at least 30 minutes (it will approximately double in size during that time). Turn out onto a table dusted with flour, knead the dough and shape into your desired loaf.

Place the dough into the loaf pan. Score the dough 4–5 times along the top and leave to rise for a further 30 minutes.

Preheat the oven to 200°C (400°C) Gas 6.

Brush the tops of the loaf with egg and add a scattering of caraway seeds to the top. Bake for 30 minutes in the preheated oven or until well risen and golden brown in colour.

Note: I usually place an ovenproof bowl of water in the oven during baking to ensure a good crust.

SEEDED RYE ROLLS

Scandinavians do love bread rolls in the morning, especially the Danes. I make these at home a lot on weekends for breakfast for my family. We freeze leftover rolls and use them for packed lunches, too, as the kids love them (and frankly, any excuse to avoid mass-produced bread). Lots of seeds and rye kernels give these rolls a nice healthy edge, but the mixture of wheat and rye ensures the rolls stay soft. Try filling these rolls with smoked salmon and cream cheese.

100 g/½ cup chopped rye kernels/rye berries

100 g/¾ cup sunflower seeds (save 50 g/⅓ cup for topping)

100 g/¾ cup pumpkin seeds (save 50g/⅓ cup for topping)

50 g/¼ cup flaxseeds/linseeds

13 g/2½ teaspoons dried/active dry yeast or 25 g/1 oz. fresh yeast *(see below)

100 ml/7 tablespoons finger-warm water (36–37°C/ 97–98°F)

250 ml/1 cup buttermilk

4 teaspoons vegetable oil

2 teaspoons salt

2 teaspoons barley malt syrup

200 g/1½ cups wholegrain rye flour

500 g/3½ cups white strong/bread flour (hold back a bit)

egg or water, for brushing

2 baking sheets greased and lined with baking parchment

MAKES 18

*If using fresh yeast, add it to the water and buttermilk and stir to dissolve.

Place the rye kernels/rye berries, sunflower seeds, pumpkin seeds and flaxseeds/linseeds in a saucepan. Cover with water, bring to the boil and allow to boil for a few minutes. Pour into a sieve/strainer, run cold water through to cool, then press out the excess water.

If using dried/active dry yeast, pour the finger-warm water into a bowl, sprinkle on the yeast and whisk. Cover with clingfilm/plastic wrap and leave in a warm place for 15 minutes to activate. Gently warm the buttermilk to finger-warm. Pour the buttermilk and yeast into a mixing bowl. Add the oil, salt and syrup and stir, then add all the rye flour and mix well. Add the rye kernels/rye berries and seeds, then slowly start adding the strong/bread flour (you may not need to add all of it). Keep kneading for about 5 minutes in a machine (longer if by hand). The dough should be a bit sticky, but stretchy. Cover the bowl with clingfilm/plastic wrap or a dish towel and leave to rise for about 1 hour or until it has doubled in size.

On a floured surface, tip out the dough and knead it through. Make sure it is nice and elastic at this stage – if not, add a bit more flour. Using your hands or a rolling pin, roll the dough to a 20 x 45-cm/ 8 x 17-in. rectangle. Carefully move the dough to one side, spread one-third of the reserved seeds on the table and lay the dough back over. Lightly brush the surface with egg or water, scatter the remaining seeds on top and press gently into the dough. Using a dough or pizza cutter, cut the rectangle into 18 equal squares.

Preheat the oven to 180°C (350°F) Gas 4. Place the rolls (well spread out) on the baking sheets. Leave to rise again for 20 minutes, covered with clingfilm/plastic wrap. Bake for around 15 minutes. Remove from the oven and leave to cool.

'SEMLOR' LENT BUNS

Every January, the excitement builds because our customers know it is almost time for 'Semlor' buns. Scandinavians celebrate the start of Lent in different ways, but all of us like to eat as many of these addictive treats as physically possible (rumour has it there are no calories in Semlor if you eat them with your eyes closed).

13 g/2½ teaspoons dried/active dry yeast or 25 g/1 oz. fresh yeast *(see below)

250 ml/1 cup whole milk, heated to 36-37°C (97-98°F)

80 g/¾ stick butter, melted and cooled slightly

40 g/3¼ tablespoons caster/granulated sugar

300-400 g/2-3 cups white strong/bread flour

½ teaspoon salt

1 teaspoon baking powder

2 teaspoons ground cardamom

1 egg, lightly beaten

FILLING:

100 g/3½ oz. marzipan/almond paste (see page 110)

good dollop of custard or Crème Pâtissière (see page 113)

500 ml/2 cups whipping cream

1 teaspoon vanilla sugar

icing/confectioners' sugar, to dust

piping bag fitted with a plain nozzle/tip

MAKES 12

*If using fresh yeast, add it to the finger-warm milk and mix until dissolved. Then pour it into the bowl of a food mixer fitted with a dough hook attachment.

If using dried/active dy yeast, sprinkle the yeast granules into the finger-warm milk and whisk together. Cover with clingfilm/plastic wrap and leave in a warm place for about 15 minutes to activate and become frothy and bubbly. Pour into the bowl of a food mixer with a dough hook and stir in the melted butter. Add the sugar and stir again. Add half of the flour as well as the salt, baking powder and ground cardamom. Add half the beaten egg (reserve the other half for brushing before baking).

Mix well until all the ingredients are incorporated and then start to add more of the flour, bit by bit, until you have a dough that is only a little bit sticky. Take care not to add too much flour. Knead the dough for at least 5 minutes in the mixer. Cover the bowl with a dish towel or clingfilm/plastic wrap and leave to rise in a warm (not hot) place until it has doubled in size - about 30-40 minutes.

Turn the dough out to a floured surface. Knead again for a few minutes, adding more flour if needed. You want a firmer but not dry dough. Cut the dough into 12 equal-sized pieces. Place, evenly spaced, on a baking sheet. Leave to rise for 25-30 minutes.

Preheat the oven to 200°C (400°F) Gas 6.

Brush each bun with the beaten egg and bake for 8-10 minutes or until baked through - keep an eye on them as they can burn quickly. Remove from oven and cover the buns with a lightly damp dish towel immediately - this will prevent them from forming a crust.

When they have cooled completely, cut a 'lid' off the buns - about 1.5 cm/½ in. from the top. Scoop out about one-third of the inside of the bun and place this in a separate bowl. Mix it with the marzipan/almond paste until it forms a very sticky mass - add a dollop of custard or Crème Pâtissière at this point to help it along. You want a spoonable, even mixture. Spoon the filling back into the buns, equally divided.

Whip the cream with the vanilla sugar until stiff, then use a piping bag fitted with a plain nozzle/tip to pipe cream on all the buns. Put the 'lids' back on and dust lightly with icing/confectioners' sugar.

NORDIC GINGER BISCUITS

**It's not Christmas without each Scandinavian
person consuming a mountain of these biscuits!
It's such fun to make these with the kids, and
really get into the festive mood together.**

550 g/4 cups plain/
all-purpose flour

1 teaspoon bicarbonate of/
baking soda

1 teaspoon ground ginger

1 teaspoon ground cloves

2 teaspoons ground cinnamon

1 teaspoon ground cardamom

pinch of ground allspice

pinch of salt

150 g/1 stick plus
2 tablespoons butter,
room temperature

200 g/10 tablespoons
golden/light corn syrup

100 g/½ cup granulated sugar

100 g/½ cup dark brown sugar

150 ml/½ cup double/heavy
cream

½ teaspoon orange zest

icing/confectioners' sugar,
to dust

MAKES 50–70

Mix the flour and
bicarbonate of/baking soda with the
dry spices and salt. Add the butter and all the
other ingredients and mix until you have an even
dough. It may still be sticky, but shape into a log and wrap in
clingfilm/plastic wrap and leave to rest in the fridge overnight
before using. Try to resist eating the dough every time you pass
by the fridge. Yes, we know it is hard not to do!

Preheat the oven to 200°C (400°F) Gas 6.

Roll out the dough thinly on a floured surface and use cookie
cutters to cut your desired shapes. You want the biscuits/cookies
to be thin.

Bake in the preheated oven on lined baking sheets – each batch
will take 5–6 minutes depending on the thickness. You want the
biscuits/cookies to be a darker shade of brown .

Remove from the oven and cool on a cooling rack. Dust with
icing/confectioners' sugar
and serve or keep in an
airtight container.

CHRISTMAS (JUL)

Christmas or 'Jul' is every Nordic person's treasured time of the year. It may be dark almost all of the time during the winter months, but in our hearts, there's so much warmth and light and enough comfort to fend off the cold snowy weather outside. At the café, this is by far our favourite time of year. We get to help hoards of homesick Scandinavians create a real Nordic Christmas in the UK – and a time when we get to show everybody else all the delicious treats we enjoy in the month leading up to Jul.

While the snow falls and the days are as dark and short as they can be, Scandinavians fill December with magic and tradition. At this time of year, we all believe in 'Tomte' or 'Nisse' – the little Christmas gnomes from Scandinavian folklore (if you're Icelandic, you have 13 little Christmas gnomes to keep track of or you won't get any presents!).

The first Sunday of Advent usually marks the start of the Christmas season and festive cheer. These four Advent Sundays are also for hosting or attending Glögg Parties – visiting friends and family, sipping delicious Glögg (mulled wine) and eating sweet homemade treats. Depending on the country and region, we make and bake anything from ginger biscuits to marzipan treats, saffron buns and every other old family Christmas recipe imaginable.

Luciadagen (St. Lucia's Day) is celebrated all over Scandinavia on 13th December. The tradition has both Pagan and Christian roots: firstly, it was the day of the Pagan festival 'Lussinatt', the darkest night of the year, when spirits, gnomes and trolls roamed the earth. Lussi, a feared enchantress, punished anyone who dared work. Legend also has it that farm animals talked to each other on this night. On this magical night, we drive the evil spirits away with candles and singing in the darkness. Secondly, this day was also the feast of the Christian St. Lucia of Syracuse (who died in the year 304). This day also coincided with the Winter Solstice, the shortest day of the year before calendar reforms, so her feast day became a festival of light across Scandinavia.

Scandinavians don't start the celebrations too early, though, and Christmas trees at home aren't usually put up until just before the big day. We celebrate Christmas on Christmas Eve with close family – giving and receiving presents and even dancing around the tree. Christmas Day is usually a calm day with a relaxed family lunch.

GLÖGG (NORDIC MULLED WINE)

Glögg is an essential part of Christmas all over Scandinavia. It's enjoyed throughout the cold months and especially on Sundays in Advent leading up to Christmas. Glögg tends to be traditionally mulled with cinnamon, cardamom, cloves and dried orange peel. This is recipe is borrowed from my sister-in-law Annika, who makes bottles and bottles of this in her Gothenburg kitchen every December. We love having a café full of people drinking hot wine and eating ginger biscuits – the aroma is amazing and it promotes a lovely atmosphere of 'hygge' and chit chat.

1 x 70-cl/24-fl. oz. bottle red wine (the quality doesn't matter)

1-2 cinnamon sticks

1 teaspoon dried root ginger

1 teaspoon dried Seville orange peel (or other orange peel if you can't get Seville)

7 whole cardamom pods

15-16 whole cloves

80 g/⅓ cup plus 1 tablespoon caster/ granulated sugar

flaked/slivered almonds and raisins, to serve

SERVES 4

Pour the wine into a saucepan, add the rest of the ingredients and heat to around 75–80°C (165–170°F), stirring to dissolve the sugar. Be careful not to heat it above 80°C (170°F) degrees, or the alcohol will start to evaporate. Remove the saucepan from the heat and leave to infuse for at least 1 hour, longer if possible.

Strain the mixture and return the mulled wine to the bottle (use a funnel to make life easier for yourself). The Glögg can be kept for at least a week.

To serve, pour the wine into a saucepan and heat it up (again, take care not to let it boil). Place a few flaked/slivered almonds and raisins in the bottom of your serving cups, and pour the Glögg over the mixture.

If you want to give your Glögg an extra kick, add a splash of either vodka, aquavit, rum or cognac to the bottom of the cups just before you pour in the Glögg.

CINNAMON WREATH WITH RYE

I sometimes make this when I need a centrepiece for a big fika session or birthday party. Essentially, a big cinnamon bun with a bit of extra oomph.

DOUGH:

25 g/1 oz. fresh yeast or 13 g/2½ teaspoons dried/active dry yeast

80 g/5½ tablespoons butter, melted

300 ml/1¼ cups whole milk, at room temperature

50 g/¼ cup sugar

2 teaspoons ground cardamom

375 g/3 cups white strong/bread flour

80 g/¾ cup rye flour

½ teaspoon salt

½ beaten egg

FILLING:

100 g/7 tablespoons butter (spreadable)

3 teaspoons ground cinnamon

1 teaspoon ground cardamom

125 g/generous ⅔ cup dark brown sugar

25 g/2 tablespoons caster/granulated sugar

70 g/½ cup chopped toasted nuts, e.g. almonds and hazelnuts

TOPPING & BRUSHING:

½ beaten egg mixed with a dash of milk, for brushing

Syrup (see page 150)

icing/confectioners' sugar and warm water (see right)

piping bag fitted with a plain nozzle/tip

SERVES 10-12

If using fresh yeast, pour the melted butter into the milk. The temperature should be between 36–37°C (97–98°F). Add the yeast and stir until dissolved. Pour into a mixing bowl.

If using dried/active dry yeast, heat the milk to 36–37°C (97–98°F) and pour it into a bowl. Sprinkle in the yeast granules and whisk together. Cover with clingfilm/plastic wrap and leave in a warm place for 15 minutes to activate. Pour the mixture into a mixing bowl. Add the melted butter, sugar and cardamom and stir again. Add 250 g/1¾ cups strong/bread flour and all the rye flour, salt and egg. Mix until everything is incorporated. Work the dough until it almost stops sticking and has a shiny surface – about 5 minutes with a mixer using a dough hook, or 10 minutes by hand. The dough should only just reach the point of not being sticky. Leave to rise until it's doubled (around 40 minutes).

To make the filling, put the softened butter, cinnamon, cardamom and sugars into a bowl and mix well.

Tip the dough out on a floured surface and work it with your hands, adding more flour, until you have a good, mouldable dough that does not stick and can be rolled out. Cut the dough in half and roll each piece in a rectangular shape (around 50 cm x 40 cm/16 x 20 in.). Spread the butter mixture evenly across the dough. Add three-quarters of the chopped nuts across the surface. Roll the dough up lengthways so you end up with a long, tight roll. Place on a baking sheet and shape into a round circle, attaching the ends. Using scissors, cut slices almost to the base. Spread each roll out to the side and flatten slightly until you have done the whole wreath. Ensure the wreath is quite flat. Let the wreath rest again for 30 minutes under a clean dish towel.

Preheat the oven to 200°C (400°F) Gas 6. Brush the wreath gently with the remaining egg/milk and bake in the preheated oven for 20-25 minutes or until done.

Brush at once with a very thin layer of warmed syrup, then sprinkle over the rest of the nuts and keep under a damp dish towel until cooled a bit. Once cooled, make the icing using a little icing/confectioners' sugar and a few drops of warm water and pipe over the wreath.

LUCIA CELEBRATION SAFFRON BUNS

Scandinavians celebrate St. Lucia's Day on 13th December – the day we wake up early and sing the light into the darkness. Processions of children in white robes tied with red sashes walk through towns holding candles. At the front, a girl – the Lucia Bride – wears a wreath of real candles in her hair. In Sweden and Norway, saffron bread and buns are traditionally eaten on this day. We also enjoy these buns at our famous Glögg parties.

50 g/3 tablespoons fresh yeast or 25 g/1 oz. dried/active dry yeast

400 ml/1¾ cups whole milk, heated to 36–37°C (97–99°F)

1 g/1 teaspoon saffron powder (if using saffron strands, grind to a powder in a pestle and mortar and soak in the milk beforehand)

150 g/¾ cup caster/granulated sugar

200 g/1 cup plain skyr, quark or Greek yogurt, at room temperature

1 teaspoon salt

1 egg

175 g/1½ sticks butter, softened, at room temperature

approx. 800 g/5¾ cups white strong/bread flour

handful of raisins

beaten egg, for brushing

3–4 large baking sheets, greased and lined with baking parchment

MAKES 30

If using fresh yeast, add the yeast and milk to a mixer with a dough hook attached. Mix until the yeast has dissolved, then add the saffron powder.

If using dried/active dry yeast pour milk into a bowl, sprinkle in the yeast and whisk together. Cover with clingfilm/plastic wrap and leave in a warm place for about 15 minutes to activate and become frothy and bubbly. Add the saffron powder. Pour into a mixer with a dough hook attached.

Add the sugar and mix together for a minute or so, then add skyr, quark or Greek yogurt, salt and egg, and mix well. Gradually add the softened butter in pieces and begin to add the flour gradually while mixing, making sure there are no lumps of butter. You'll need around 800 g/5¾ cups or so of flour, but the exact amount depends on how the dough feels. Keep mixing until you have a dough that is still sticky, but doesn't stick to your finger too much when you poke it. Too much flour makes the buns dry. If you're using an electric mixer, knead for about 5 minutes or knead by hand for 10 minutes. Leave the dough to rise in a warm place until it has doubled in size (about 30–40 minutes in a bowl covered with clingfilm/plastic wrap).

Turn the dough out on a lightly floured surface and knead until smooth. Cut the dough into 30 equal-sized pieces. Roll each piece in your hand into a long cylinder, then transfer to the baking sheets and mould into an 'S' shape (see picture opposite). Add a single raisin to the centre of the point where the 'S' shape curves (two raisins for each bun). Leave to rise again for 25 minutes.

Preheat the oven to 200°C (400°F) Gas 6.

Brush gently with egg and bake them in the preheated oven for 10–12 minutes. The buns should have a slight tinge of brown on top.

Leave to cool under a damp dish towel (this prevents them from becoming dry).

REAL CINNAMON BUNS

We like this recipe because it's simple, straightforward and it just works. Along with that, it is pretty traditional and doesn't try to be something it is not. Why complicate a simple, good thing?

1 x quantity Dough
(see page 150)

plain/all-purpose flour, to
dust the work surface

FILLING:

80 g/½ stick plus
1 tablespoon butter,
at room temperature

1 teaspoon plain/all-purpose
flour

1 tablespoon ground cinnamon

½ teaspoon ground
cardamom

½ teaspoon vanilla sugar

80 g/¼ cup plus 2
tablespoons sugar

egg, for brushing

TOPPING:

Syrup (see page 150)

nibbed 'pearl' sugar
or chopped, toasted nuts

*2 baking sheets, greased and
lined with baking parchment*

MAKES 16

Dust the table top with flour and turn out the dough. Knead the dough with your hands and work in more flour if needed. Using a rolling pin, roll out the dough to a 40 x 50 cm/16 x 20 in. rectangle.

In a bowl, add the butter, spices and sugars and mix together well. Using a spatula, spread the mixture evenly over the rolled-out dough. Carefully roll the dough lengthways into a long roll. Using a sharp knife, cut 16 slices.

Place the swirls onto the baking sheets (not too close as they will rise further). Leave to prove under a dish towel for 30 minutes.

Preheat the oven to 200°C (400°F) Gas 6.

Brush each bun lightly with egg and pop the buns into the preheated oven to bake for around 10–12 minutes. Watch the buns as they bake: they can go dark very quickly and you may also need to move the buns around in the oven if they are not baking evenly.

When golden, remove from the oven. Brush the buns lightly with the warmed syrup then decorate with the nibbed 'pearl' sugar or chopped, toasted nuts. Immediately place a damp, clean dish towel on top for a few minutes to prevent the buns from going dry.

The secret to making the best cinnamon buns? Love. Lots of it. Knead the love into the dough.

NORWEGIAN CREAM BUNS

This is the ultimate comfort bun for Norwegians. Traditionally named 'Skoleboller' ('school buns'), we call them Norwegian cream buns at the café.

1 x quantity of Dough
(see page 150)

½ quantity of Crème Pâtissière
(see page 113)

1 beaten egg, for brushing

150 g/1 cup icing/
confectioners' sugar

50 g/²⁄₃ cup desiccated/dried
shredded coconut

MAKES 14

Follow the recipe on page 150 to make the dough.

After the dough has risen, roll out the dough into a cylinder and cut it into 14 pieces. Roll each piece into a neat circle, then place on a baking sheet and flatten firmly (although they will spring back into place after a while). Make sure you space the buns out evenly.

Using the base of a glass measuring around 4–5 cm/1½–2 in. in diameter, press down the middle of each bun and add a good tablespoon of Crème Pâtissière to each indentation.

Leave the buns to rise for a further 20 minutes.

Preheat the oven to 200°C (400°F) Gas 6.

Lightly brush the buns with egg (avoid the custard centres) and bake in the preheated oven for around 10 minutes, or until done (times may vary depending on your oven).

Cover the baked buns with a damp dish towel for 5–10 minutes as soon as you have removed them from the oven to avoid a crust forming.

Once the buns have cooled, make the icing/frosting. Add a few tablespoons of hot water to the icing/confectioners' sugar and stir. Keep adding water, drop by drop, and stirring until you have a smooth consistency that can be stirred but is still thick, like a syrup.

Using a plastic pastry brush or a palette knife, carefully smooth the icing/frosting on top of all the buns, avoiding the cream centre. After each bun has been brushed, sprinkle coconut over the top.

VANILLA AND CARDAMOM KNOTS

A fresh take on the Swedish cinnamon bun, without the cinnamon.

13 g/2½ teaspoons
dried/active dry yeast or
25 g/1 oz. fresh yeast
*(see below)

250 ml/1 cup whole milk,
heated to 36-37°C (97-99°F)

80 g/¾ stick butter, melted
and cooled slightly

40 g/3 tablespoons
caster/granulated sugar

400-500 g/3-3⅔ cups
white strong/bread flour

2 teaspoons ground
cardamom

1 teaspoon salt

1 egg, beaten

flaked/slivered almonds,
to decorate

FILLING:

100 g/7 tablespoons butter,
at room temperature

50 g/¼ cup sugar

1-2 teaspoons vanilla sugar or
extract (or use the seeds from
1 vanilla pod/bean)

1 teaspoon ground cardamom

80 g/3 oz. marzipan/almond
paste (see page 110), chopped
(optional)

SYRUP:

3 tablespoons golden/light
corn syrup and 6 tablespoons
water, heated in a saucepan

*2 baking sheets, greased and
lined with baking parchment*

MAKES 16

*If using fresh yeast, add the
warm milk to a mixing bowl
and add the yeast; stir until
dissolved, then pour into the
bowl of the food mixer.

Pour the warm milk into a bowl, sprinkle in the yeast and whisk together. Cover with clingfilm/plastic wrap and leave in a warm place for about 15 minutes to become bubbly. Pour into the bowl of a food mixer fitted with a dough hook. Start the machine and add the cooled, melted butter. Allow to combine with the yeast for 1 minute or so, then add the sugar. Allow to combine for 1 minute.

In a separate bowl, weigh out 400 g/3 cups of the flour, add the cardamom and salt and mix together. Start adding the flour and spices into the milk mixture, bit by bit. Add half the beaten egg. Keep kneading for 5 minutes. You may need to add more flour – you want the mixture to end up a bit sticky, but not so much that it sticks to your finger if you poke it. It is better not to add too much flour as this will result in dry buns. You can always add more later.

Once mixed, leave the dough in a bowl and cover with a dish towel or clingfilm/plastic wrap. Allow to rise for around 30 minutes or until it has doubled in size.

Dust a table top with flour and turn out the dough. Using your hands, knead the dough and work in more flour if needed. Using a rolling pin, roll out the dough to a 40 x 50 cm/16 x 20 in. rectangle.

To make the filling, place the butter in a bowl and add the sugar, vanilla sugar or extract and cardamom and mix well. Using a spatula, spread the butter evenly over the rolled-out dough. Sprinkle the marzipan/almond paste (if using) over the filling, then fold half the dough on top of the other, lengthways (you will end up with a 20 x 50-cm/8 x 20-in rectangle). Using a knife or pizza cutter, cut 16 widthways strips of dough. Carefully take one strip and twist it a few times, then roll into a 'knot', carefully ensuring both ends are under or inside the bun so they do not spring open during baking. Place each bun on the baking sheet and leave to prove under a dish towel for another 30 minutes.

Preheat the oven to 200°C (400°F) Gas 6.

Brush each bun lightly with the remaining beaten egg and bake in the preheated oven for 10-12 minutes. Watch the buns as they bake: they can go dark very quickly and you may also need to move the buns around in the oven if they are not baking evenly. When golden, remove from the oven and immediately place a damp clean dish towel on top for a few minutes to prevent the buns from going dry. Brush the warm syrup lightly over the buns and decorate with flaked/slivered almonds.

Northern Scandinavia is one of the most stunning places on earth, especially in the winter.

FIKA

Meeting up for coffee and something sweet is one of the most important events in Scandinavia. We do this several times a day. It is as much about the coffee and cake as it is about taking time out to sit down, have a break and share words and cake with someone you like – whether it's with family, friends or colleagues. There are many fika cakes across Scandinavia – here I have chosen some of the café favourites to share with you.

CHOCOLATE BISCUIT SLICES

These moreish biscuits/cookies are easy to make and bake in super-quick time – the perfect accompaniment to a cup of coffee.

100 g/1 stick minus
1 tablespoon butter

80 g/⅓ cup caster/
granulated sugar

2 teaspoons vanilla sugar

1 teaspoon golden syrup/light
corn syrup

150 g/1 cup plain/all-purpose
flour

4 teaspoons cacao or cocoa
powder

1 teaspoon baking powder

pearl sugar or chopped
almonds, to decorate

*2 baking sheets, greased and
lined with baking parchment*

MAKES APPROX. 24

Preheat the oven to 180°C (350°F) Gas 4.

In a bowl, cream together the butter, caster/granulated sugar and vanilla sugar. Add the syrup and mix well. In a separate bowl, sift the dry ingredients together, then mix into the wet mixture. Bring the mixture together with your hands to form an even dough – it should not be sticky.

Split the dough into two lumps. Roll out each lump into a 6 x 35 cm/ 2½ x 14 in. rectangle, directly on the prepared baking sheets.

Sprinkle the pearl sugar or chopped almonds down the middle of the dough, then bake in the preheated oven for about 10 minutes until almost baked through. As soon as you remove them from the oven, use a pizza wheel or sharp knife to cut each piece into 12 even-sized strips.

Leave to cool on a wire rack and store in an airtight container for up to a week.

TOFFEE BISCUIT SLICES

A Swedish classic, these toffee biscuits/cookies are super-quick to make. We like adding flakes of sea salt to the top, but you can easily leave this out, if you wish.

140 g/1¼ sticks butter

120 g/½ cup caster/
granulated sugar

4 tablespoons golden syrup/
light corn syrup

1½ teaspoons vanilla sugar

1 teaspoon baking powder

300 g/2¼ cups plain/all-
purpose flour

½ teaspoon sea salt (I use
Malden), optional

*3 baking sheets, greased and
lined with baking parchment*

MAKES APPROX. 36

Preheat the oven to 180°C (350°F) Gas 4.

In a bowl, cream the butter and caster/granulated sugar until pale and fluffy, then add the syrup, followed by the vanilla sugar, baking powder and flour. Mix with your hands until you have an even dough.

Cut the dough into 3 equal pieces. Roll out to the size of 6 x 35 cm/ 2½ x 14 in. directly on the prepared baking sheets. Sprinkle the salt over the top of the dough, if using.

Bake in the preheated oven for 8–10 minutes. As soon as you remove the biscuits/cookies from oven, use a pizza wheel or sharp knife to cut each rectangle into 12 pieces.

Leave to cool on a wire rack and store in an airtight container for up to a week.

SUPER-EASY CHOCOLATE OAT TREATS

All children in Scandinavia know how to make these. Simply the easiest no-bake treat to make – and utterly delicious to snack on. If you prefer less coffee flavour, you can leave it out and add a dash of milk or chocolate milk instead.

250 g/2¼ sticks butter

400 g/4 cups rolled oats

175 g/¾ cup caster/
granulated sugar

4 tablespoons cocoa powder

4 tablespoons strong, cooled
coffee

1 teaspoon vanilla sugar

desiccated/dried shredded
coconut, sugar sprinkles or
pearl sugar, to decorate

MAKES APPROX. 40

Blitz all the ingredients, except the coconut, sugar sprinkles or
pearl sugar in a food processor or mix by hand (but allow the
butter to soften before doing so).

Put the mixture in the fridge to firm up a bit before using or it can
be a bit too sticky. Add more oats if you feel the mixture is too soft.

Roll into 2.5-cm/1-in. diameter balls, then roll each ball in either
desiccated/dried shredded coconut, sugar sprinkles or pearl sugar.

Firm up in the fridge before eating – they will keep for up to a week
in the fridge.

NORDIC OAT CRISP BISCUITS

A simple, quick, tasty treat and one of the more traditional Swedish fika biscuits.

180 g/1 cup caster/granulated
sugar

2 eggs

1 generous tablespoon
plain/all-purpose flour

1 teaspoon baking powder

100 g/1 cup rolled oats

20 g/1½ tablespoons rye
flakes (or plain rolled oats)

a pinch of salt

a drop of vanilla extract

50 g/3½ tablespoons butter,
melted

50 g/2 oz. dark/bittersweet
chocolate, melted

*2 baking sheets, greased and
lined with baking parchment*

MAKES APPROX. 30

In a bowl, whisk the sugar and eggs until fluffy. In a separate bowl,
sift together the flour and baking powder, then mix into the sugar
and egg mixture with the oats, rye flakes (or extra oats), salt and
vanilla. Stir together well. Pour in the melted butter, stirring until
well combined. Leave for 15 minutes before using.

Preheat the oven to 200°C (400°F) Gas 6.

Drop tablespoons of the mixture onto the prepared baking sheets,
leaving at least 5 cm/1 in. between the biscuits as they will spread
out a lot during baking.

Bake in the preheated oven for 5 minutes – the biscuits are done
once they have a slight brown colour. Remove from oven, then
transfer with a spatula to a cold surface to cool.

Decorate the biscuits with lines of melted chocolate. Leave to dry,
then store in an airtight container.

DANISH DREAM CAKE

This Danish Dream Cake (or 'Drømmekage fra Brovst') originates from Brovst, a village in Jutland. In 1965, a young girl baked her grandmother's secret family recipe in a competition and won, and the cake has been a favourite of all Danes ever since. No wonder: it's light and fluffy with a delicious coconut topping.

3 eggs

225 g/1 cup caster/granulated sugar

½ teaspoon vanilla sugar

225 g/1¾ cups plain/all-purpose flour or cake flour

2 teaspoons baking powder

150 ml/⅔ cup whole milk

75 g/¾ stick butter, melted

TOPPING:

100 g/1 stick butter

150 g/1½ cups desiccated/dried shredded coconut

250 g/1¼ cups dark brown sugar

75 ml/⅓ cup whole milk

a pinch of salt

a 23-cm/9-in. springform or round cake pan, greased and lined with baking parchment

SERVES 10–12

Preheat the oven to 190°C (375°F) Gas 5.

In the bowl of a food mixer, whisk the eggs, caster/granulated sugar and vanilla sugar on a high speed for a few minutes, until white and light. Meanwhile, in a separate bowl, sift the flour and baking powder together.

Carefully fold the flour into the egg mixture. Mix the milk with the melted butter in a jug/pitcher and carefully pour into the batter, folding it in until incorporated. Pour the batter into the prepared cake pan.

Bake in the preheated oven for 35–40 minutes, or until almost done (try not to open the oven door for the first 20 minutes of the total baking time).

To make the topping, put all the ingredients in a saucepan and gently melt together.

Remove the cake from the oven and carefully spread the topping all over the cake. Return to the oven. Turn up the heat to 200°C (400°F) Gas 6 and bake for a further 5 minutes.

Leave cake to cool before eating, if you can (we are well aware it's hard to do that).

This is baked in all Danish households. It's a true Danish classic, and the topping is utterly delicious.

FIKA AND HYGGE

Scandinavians love to meet up for coffee, cake and a chat - and in Sweden there is a word to describe just that: fika. It's used both as a noun and a verb. You can *fika* all throughout the day or you can meet up for a *fika*. Fika can be a few minutes to several hours long. You can do it with family, friends or have daily fika-breaks at work with your colleagues. You can even have a fika-date (which tends to involve a lot less pressure than a formal date, plus you won't have to buy a new dress).

When you fika, it usually involves meeting up, drinking coffee and eating something baked – the most famous of which is the cinnamon bun. However, there are many different types of fika cakes and even fika sweet bread and buns. Cakes such as green marzipan 'Princess Cake' and easy coffee treats such as 'Dammsugare' are firm fika favourites, both across Scandinavia and in our café in London. At ScandiKitchen, we start every day with a huge batch of warm cinnamon buns right out of the oven. People pop by from the early morning to sit down and have a bun and a cup of coffee and fika for a while before work. In the afternoons, we are full with the hustle and bustle of people meeting up again for more coffee and a slice of home-baked 'Dream Cake' or 'Kladdkaka' or any of the other many varieties we make. Come weekends, the café is full of people fika'ing.

Back in the 1940s in Sweden, a book was published called *Sju Sorter Kakor* (Seven Kinds of Cakes). When receiving visitors, it was customary for the lady of the house to offer no less than seven different types of biscuits or cakes - and this book (still reprinted annually despite every household having at least three hand-me-down copies on the book shelf), features recipes for all the old best-loved cakes and biscuits, the way Grandmother baked them. Nowadays, it is no longer expected that you bake for hours before people pop over for a coffee. In southern parts of Denmark, they took it one step further: there, a traditional coffee table featured no fewer than seven types of hard cakes (biscuits) and seven types of soft cakes, too. Luckily, these days, a Southern Jutland coffee and cake table is only served on special occasions.

In Denmark, when you meet up for coffee, you also 'hygge'. Hygge is a word that cannot be translated easily, although 'an elevated state of coziness' probably comes closest. You can 'hygge' with friends, family or even alone (by candlelight or in front of the fire place, wearing slippers). Hygge refers to the warm, happy feeling you get when you are surrounded by lovely people you care about. To hygge, you need hyggelige things around you – blankets, candles, comfort food, an open fire or whatever else makes you feel all cozy and warm inside.

The high season for hygge is Christmas, but generally, we do it all year round and more often than not, there's food involved. The word originated in the 18th century in Norway where it meant 'well being', but has been adopted into Danish and is now a huge part of Danish culture and identity (although in Norway, the word for hygge is now 'koselig' – and is also a huge part of Norwegian life). Read any tourist brochure about Denmark and Norway, and hygge/kos will certainly feature as one of the things that make us who we are.

Fika: to meet up for a cup of coffee and something sweet and a 'hygge' chat.

'KÄRLEKSMUMS' LOVE CAKE

This cake has many, many names across Scandinavia. We call it Love Cake (from the Swedish 'kärlek' meaning 'love' and 'mums' meaning 'something delicious'). We changed the traditional chocolate sponge at the café to a darker chocolate cake as we feel it goes better with the mocha icing.

50 g/scant $\frac{1}{2}$ cup cacao or cocoa powder

100 ml/$\frac{1}{3}$ cup whole milk

175 g/1$\frac{1}{2}$ sticks butter

225 g/1 cup granulated sugar

2 eggs

225 g/1$\frac{3}{4}$ cups plain/all-purpose flour or cake flour

1 teaspoon vanilla sugar or extract

1 teaspoon bicarbonate of/baking soda

$\frac{1}{2}$ teaspoon salt

TOPPING:

150 g/1 cup icing/confectioners' sugar, sifted

50 g/3$\frac{1}{2}$ tablespoons butter

1 generous tablespoon cacao or cocoa powder

$\frac{1}{2}$ teaspoon vanilla sugar

4 tablespoons strong filter coffee

50 g/$\frac{3}{4}$ cup desiccated/dried shredded coconut, plus extra to decorate

coarse sea salt, to decorate

a 22-cm/9-in. deep round cake pan, greased and lined with baking parchment

SERVES 8–10

Preheat the oven to 180°C (350°F) Gas 4.

In a bowl, mix together the cacao or cocoa with 100 ml/$\frac{1}{3}$ cup of boiling water to make a paste and leave to cool. Gradually pour in the milk and stir well until combined and smooth.

In a separate bowl, cream together the butter and caster/granulated sugar until pale and fluffy. Add the eggs one by one, mixing well between each addition and taking care that they are completely incorporated.

In a third bowl, sift together the flour, vanilla sugar or extract, bicarbonate of/baking soda and salt.

Add the flour and the cacao or cocoa mixtures to the egg mixture, whisking continuously, taking care to ensure everything is well incorporated, but not over-beating or your cake will be heavy. Spoon the mixture into the prepared cake pan, spreading evenly. Bake in the middle of the preheated oven for 30–35 minutes, or until a skewer comes out just clean (take care not to over-bake).

Leave to cool slightly, then turn out onto a wire rack to cool completely.

To make the topping, put all the ingredients except the salt in a saucepan. Melt together gently, stirring until well combined. Cool, then spoon the topping onto the cooled cake and spread evenly. Decorate with the extra coconut and sea salt, then leave to set before serving.

AUNTIE INGA'S 'KLADDKAKA' STICKY CHOCOLATE CAKE

This cake is one of the most famous fika cakes in Sweden. Every café has a version of Kladdkaka (which literally means 'Sticky Cake'). It is a bit like an under-baked chocolate cake and that is exactly what makes it so very good. This is our Auntie Inga's recipe. It's an easy cake to make, but watch the baking: too little and it's a runny mess; too much and it's a stodgy, dry cake.

2 eggs

200 g/1 cup caster/granulated sugar

150 g/1 cup plain/all-purpose flour or cake flour

3 tablespoons good-quality cocoa powder (I use Fazer), plus extra for dusting

1 tablespoon vanilla sugar or extract

a pinch of salt

100 g/1 stick unsalted butter, melted and cooled slightly

whipped cream, to serve

a 20-cm/8-in. deep round cake pan, greased and lined with baking parchment

SERVES 6–8

Preheat the oven to 180°C (350°F) Gas 4.

Whisk the eggs and sugar together until the mixture is light, fluffy and pale.

Sift all the dry ingredients into the egg and sugar mixture. Fold in until everything is incorporated, then fold in the melted butter.

Pour into the prepared cake pan.

Bake in the preheated oven for around 10–15 minutes. The exact time can vary, so keep an eye on the cake. A perfect kladdkaka is very, very soft in the middle, but not runny once it has cooled – but almost runny. The cake will not rise, but it will puff up slightly during baking.

If you press down gently on the cake, the crust should need a bit of pressure to crack. When this happens, the cake is done. Leave to cool in the pan.

Serve with whipped cream, dusted with cocoa powder.

THAT CARROT CAKE

It's rare that I don't tire of a cake (trust me, I do eat a lot of cake). However, this carrot cake recipe is one that I started making over 12 years ago when I worked at innocent Drinks and we used to bring in cake every Friday for afternoon coffee breaks. It is still one of the most asked for recipes at ScandiKitchen and the first cake to sell out. Over time, the recipe has changed very little. What started out as a bet with Jonas about 'making the best carrot cake, like, ever' is still our favourite cake.

150 g/$\frac{3}{4}$ cup caster/granulated sugar

150 g/$\frac{3}{4}$ cup light brown sugar

3 eggs

300 ml/1$\frac{1}{4}$ cups sunflower oil

300 g/2$\frac{1}{3}$ cups self-raising/rising flour or 2 cups cake flour mixed with 4 teaspoons baking powder

$\frac{1}{2}$ teaspoon salt

1 teaspoon vanilla sugar

2 teaspoons ground cinnamon

1 teaspoon mixed spice/apple pie spice

300 g/3 cups grated carrots

70 g/$\frac{1}{2}$ cup pine nuts

TOPPING:

300 g/1$\frac{1}{2}$ cups cream cheese

100 g/$\frac{3}{4}$ cup icing/confectioners' sugar, sifted

50 g/3$\frac{1}{2}$ tablespoons softened butter

freshly squeezed juice of 1 large lime

grated lime zest, to decorate

2 x 20-cm/8-in. round cake pans, greased and lined with baking parchment

SERVES 8

Preheat the oven to 160°C (325°F) Gas 3.

In a bowl, whisk the caster/granulated and light brown sugars together with the eggs until light and airy, gradually adding the oil.

In a separate bowl, sift the dry ingredients together, then fold into the sugar and egg mixture. Fold in the grated carrots, reserving a little for decorating the finished cake, then the pine nuts.

Pour the mixture into the prepared cake pans and bake in the preheated oven for about 25 minutes, or until a skewer inserted into the middle comes out clean. Turn out of the pans and leave to cool completely on a wire rack.

To make the topping, beat all the ingredients together well (4–5 minutes in a food mixer).

Arrange the first cake layer on a serving plate and spread over almost half of the topping evenly. Place the second cake bottom-up (so you get a perfectly flat top on your cake) on top and spread the rest of the topping over the cake. Decorate with the reserved grated carrots and lime zest.

This is not a traditional carrot cake: it's lighter and more tangy. We get asked for the recipe all the time.

APPLE AND CINNAMON CAKE

There a many different kinds of 'Real Scandinavian' Apple Cakes out there. Truth be told, there are as many 'real recipes' for apple cakes as there are people who bake them. This is a cake my mother used to bake when I was a kid, using apples from the garden. At the café, we added a layer of crème pâtissière to it for a bit of an extra scrumptiousness. This is one of the most popular cakes at the café.

150 g/1¼ sticks butter

200 g/1 cup caster/granulated sugar

1 teaspoon vanilla sugar or extract

4 eggs

200 g/1½ cups plain/all-purpose flour or cake flour

½ teaspoon salt

1½ teaspoons baking powder

150 g/¾ cup Crème Pâtissière (see page 113)

pouring cream, to serve (optional)

TOPPING:

25 g/2 tablespoons butter

50 g/¼ cup caster/granulated sugar

2 teaspoons ground cinnamon

3 Granny Smith apples, peeled, cored and chopped into 1-cm/½-in. cubes

a sprinkling of sea salt

½ teaspoon vanilla extract

a 23-cm/9-in. springform or round cake pan, greased and lined with baking parchment

SERVES 8–10

First, make the topping. In a saucepan, melt together the butter, sugar and cinnamon and add the salt and vanilla extract. Add the chopped apple and stew for a few minutes to lightly start the cooking process, then take off the heat and allow to cool completely. This can be done a day in advance.

Preheat the oven to 175°C (350°F) Gas 4.

To make the cake, cream the butter, caster/granulated sugar and vanilla sugar or extract together in a bowl until pale and fluffy. Lightly beat the eggs in a separate bowl, then add to the butter and sugar mixture in three stages, whisking all the time. Ensure that all the egg is fully incorporated before adding more or the batter will curdle.

In a third bowl, combine flour and other dry ingredients. Sift into the wet mixture and carefully fold in until incorporated.

Pour the mixture into the prepared cake pan and spread evenly to the sides. Dollop the Crème Pâtissière on top and spread out evenly over the batter.

Using a slotted spoon, remove the apple from its syrup and scatter over the Crème Pâtissière. Reserve the syrup for drizzling over the cake once baked.

Bake in the preheated oven for around 50 minutes – it can be tricky to tell if the cake is done because the crème patisserie will remain a bit wet, but if a skewer comes out clean, it should be baked inside.

Remove from the pan and allow to cool slightly before eating.

Enjoy with cream, if you so wish – and pour over some of the leftover syrup for added oomph (I like to add a little more salt to the syrup – it really lifts it).

'DAMMSUGARE' MARZIPAN TRUFFLE TREATS

Every bakery in Sweden sells 'Dammsugare' ('vacuum cleaners'). Not real ones, mind you, but little log-shaped cakes covered with marzipan. They are called 'Dammsugare' because they used to be made using all the leftover crumbs. Making these at home is easy and, yes, you make them using leftover cake. In my house, we rarely have leftover cake so we use a store-bought sponge cake or similar, but you can mix and match leftover cakes, pastries and whatever else you have.

250 g/2½ cups crumbled leftover cake (store-bought Madeira, sponge, Swiss/jelly roll or similar)

75 g/5 tablespoons butter

1½ tablespoons cocoa powder

1 tablespoon raspberry jam/preserve

rum essence or arrack liqueur, to taste

green food colouring paste

250 g/9 oz. marzipan/almond paste (at least 25% almond content) (see page 110)

icing/confectioners' sugar, to dust

150 g/5 oz. dark/bittersweet chocolate, melted

MAKES APPROX. 60

Put the cake crumbs, butter, cocoa, raspberry jam/preserve and rum essence or arrack liqueur into a food mixer and mix on a medium setting until you have a smooth paste. Leave to rest in the fridge for an hour before rolling.

Meanwhile, add a few drops of green food colouring paste to the marzipan and work it with your hands until the colour is even.

Roll out the marzipan on a surface lightly dusted with icing/confectioners' sugar.

Roll long logs of the cake mixture, approximately 1.5 cm/⅝ in. in diameter and lay them on top of the marzipan. Roll the marzipan around the cake mixture and cut. Set aside seam-side down. Repeat until you have used all of the filling and marzipan, then cut the logs into 6–7-cm/2⅓–2¾-in. pieces.

Dip each end of the logs in the melted chocolate. Leave to set in the fridge for 30 minutes before serving.

'Dammsugare' means 'vacuum cleaner' – supposedly. This no-bake treat was traditionally made with the baker's leftover crumbs!

INDEX

ACKNOWLEDGMENTS

My husband Jonas and our daughters Astrid and Elsa for putting up with me whilst I've been writing this book. You deserve a medal.

Ryland, Peters & Small – especially Cindy, Julia, Sonya and Nathan, and to Bridget, Linda and Jack. Pete Cassidy for the most amazing photography.

Jenny Linford for encouragement and friendship. This book happened because of you. Thank you.

Everybody at ScandiKitchen: you guys make the place come alive and without you, we would not be here. Special thanks to Rebekka, Luke, Karin, Torben, Tess, Trine, Helena, Sally, Anna, Elin, Emmy, Thom, Carl, Martina, Peter Molker, Richard 'Asier' Gray, David Cross and our Lord of the Ledger: David Holberton.

David Jørgensen, Laura Thomson, Theresa Boden, Andy McLaughlin: the most wonderful friends and honest, watchful eyes. Thank you for your help and support.

Lena and Niels Blomhøj, my amazing parents (thanks for teaching me how to cook). My sisters Isabelle, Ditte, Lone, Ulla and Ginny: your recipe testing and feedback has been invaluable. Also thank you to the Aurells for their family recipes and support: Leif, Eva, Annika, Mikael, Andy and Joshua – and the Carlfalks.

Friends, testers, neighbours, excess test-food eaters: Andrew Robertson, Sandi and Debbie Toksvig, Hannah Ventura, Helle Kaiser Nielsen, Sandra and Chad, Sarah Hand, Marianne Jenkins, Sheena Skinner (Queen of North Berwick), Jennifer Hadley, Mikael and Camilla Persson, Sonny, Kobi Ruzcika (the most talented chef I've ever had the pleasure of working with). Fiona and Mandy, Michelle Sirkett, Nick and Ces, Fed and Pily. Ida Jordgubb, Karl-Gunnar the forager from Umeå (thanks for the fresh cloudberries), Birgitte Ager Mote, Louise Wisson, Anette Edvardsson and Agneta Andersson.

The biggest thank you of all goes to every one of our amazingly loyal and wonderful customers and friends who pop by and see us every day, and all you guys reading our random newsletters from afar: thank you for making ScandiKitchen happen.

And thank you, ABBA, for the music. Ha!